Praise for COMM

"This is not your daddy's motivational book. Be drawn into his world and you may learn a thing or two. With a fun & unique voice all his own, Tazz Daddy knows how to speak to his audience."
- Abiola Abrams, Author, TV Big Mouth & Media Personality

"A must read, COMMON SENSE AIN'T COMMON dares to push us beyond the break, and encourages us to grab hold onto something deeper. This book definitely challenges the reader to Dream Bigger."
- Tony A. Gaskins Jr., Author/Life Coach

"In the hallways of impactful people and men who guide the culture, Tazz Daddy is a force to be reckoned with. He brings knowledge substance and excitement to the forefront."
- STAR, Host of the Star & BucWild Morning Show

"This book has great insight … has my vote for best seller … if you don't understand common sense this book will help…"
- Grizz Chapman, Star of NBC's 30 Rock

"It's a shame that nature did not provide everyone with one additional sense – Common. This book gets people one step closer to developing the common sense they sadly weren't blessed with."
- Charlamagne Tha God, The Breakfast Club, Power 105.1 NYC

COMMON SENSE AIN'T COMMON

A Practical Guide to Getting
the Most Out of Life

Tazz Daddy

authorHOUSE®

AuthorHouse™
1663 Liberty Drive
Bloomington, IN 47403
www.authorhouse.com
Phone: 1-800-839-8640

First published by AuthorHouse 7/20/2011

ISBN: 978-1-4634-0657-8 (sc)
ISBN: 978-1-4634-0656-1 (e)

Printed in the United States of America

This book is printed on acid-free paper.

Contents

Acknowledgments

First and foremost, I'd like to thank God for showing me time and again that with faith, effort, prayer, and humility, the impossible is possible.

To my mother, Edythe Anderson: There are no words to describe what you mean to me. "Thank You" almost sounds like an insult. It does not begin to express my gratitude for all that you've given me. I am the person that I am today because of your love, kindness, discipline, and desire to make me want to strive to be the best. Thank you for always believing in me, even when I did not know how to believe in myself! I am extremely grateful for you. I love you Mom, and there is nothing you can do about it!

I'd like to thank my father, Carl Anderson, for all of his sacrifices, unconditional love and unparalleled level of Common Sense. I think about you and miss you desperately every single day. I hope that I am the kind of man you envisioned that I'd grow up to be. I strive every day, with every breath I take, to be the kind of loving servant you were. You will live forever in my heart. I love you Dad.

To my brother, Aaron: You've been a surrogate father to me. You've taught me invaluable lessons that I apply in my life to this very day. Thank you for taking me in when I had no place to go. While many people find it very easy to say how they feel, you show me that you love me with your actions and your sacrifices on my behalf. When I hear the song "Wind beneath My Wings," I can't think of a song more appropriate to express how I feel about you. You always put me first in everything, and have never asked for single thing in return. I can never repay you for your kindness. I can never repay you for your selflessness. All I can do is show the world that your sacrifices were not in vain.

To Trish, Kiarra, and AJ: I love you very much! I hope that this book shows you what God can do with someone who isn't exactly what others think he should be. I also hope it gives you insight into what it means to pursue goals, even when they may seem impossible. Over the years, I've learned to stop asking "how," and I've trusted that God wouldn't put anything on my heart that he didn't plan to help me achieve. Whatever he's given you, don't run from it, RUN TOWARDS IT!

To my loving Grandmother, "Mee Mar": As a child I held your hand, going everywhere with you. It is with such great pride that I'm able to give you my hand to hold onto when you're feeling weak. There is no way for me to tell you how happy I am that you are able to see firsthand, who I am as a man, and what I've been able to accomplish because of your love and guidance. Thank you for Peanut Butter and Jelly sandwiches, Mercurochrome®, Fletcher's Castoria®, and unconditional love.

Aunt Gigi: Thank you for Star Trek, thank you for horror movies, and most importantly, thank you for being objective and honest when I needed it the most. It's definitely not easy being the youngest; and, I think that's why we've always had a kinship. You knew what it was like to grow up as the baby in the household of spectacular people. You also knew what it was like to succeed under that pressure, and those lessons have been passed onto me from you. I love you so much!

Janay: Thank you for being everything I never knew that I always needed. Your love and support have been fuel to me when I didn't think that I could go any further. I've known you for all of my adult life, and I take great pleasure in knowing that I'm going to know you forever. I love you.

To my best friend, Jeanine: Your friendship has been invaluable. You're my sister and I can't imagine life without you. You're a blessing that I will never take for granted. Thank you for all that you've done for me. I'll try everything to be worthy of your love and friendship.

To the Daniels family, the Moncrief family, the Johnson family, and the Jolley family: Thank you for being my extended family. Thank you for being family that would never abandon me. They say that blood is thicker than water, but love is bigger than blood. In your own special way, you have given me more love, more encouragement, and more support than certain people with whom I share genetic code. For this I am eternally grateful.

To J. Taylor of http://nsydeout.com: You've seen me through some very difficult times. Thank you for your objectivity, your honesty, your fresh perspective, and your friendship. Your art is amazing, but your true talent is painting truth onto people's souls. God bless you and your ever-expanding family.

To Hurricane Dave: You said that firing me was one of the hardest things you've ever been asked to do. Rest assured you did me the Greatest Favor anyone has ever done for me. I didn't know it then, nor did I understand it, but in retrospect my mission was too big for me to be the background in anyone else's foreground. You set me free to pursue everything that I never knew I was capable of. For that I thank you. I'm proud of you & everything you've accomplished at http://perdiemcard.com.

Thanks to Ken Johnson, Kelly Mac, Lorain Ballard-Morrill and the good people at Clear Channel Radio Philadelphia for the undying support and opportunities you've given me. It means the world to me.

Thanks to everyone who has embraced me and encouraged me through Blog Talk Radio! Thanks to Stephanie Tru, Ronin Martin, T. Smitty and others for your undying support.

To Fonzworth Bentley: Thank you for your prayers, your consistency, and your brilliant advice. You helped me when my faith was wavering. For that I will always be grateful. It is my sincere hope that people understand that you are more than just your fashion sense. You are an incredible human being, and an amazing artist. My prayer is that you continue to grow, as you become a blessing to the world.

To Mr. Rodney Perry: When I first told you that I was writing this book, you told me, "I hope you're prepared for the journey you're going to take. What you're about to do is going to change the world!" To be honest, I didn't believe you. Most importantly I don't think I believed in me that much. You never wavered, and I thank you!

To Headkrack at http://krackblog.com: Thank you for being a true friend to me, even when other people would have preferred that you cast me aside. Thanks for helping me when I couldn't help myself.

Thank you to the group Pretty Ricky and Uncle Blue: For feeding me and truly showing me that friendship is more important than business.

To Tangie Larkin & Maria More: You two are some of the most positive women I've ever met! Thank you for your support. Thank you for your contributions. Thank you for your undying friendship whether I was up, or whether I was down. Your belief in me is immeasurable to say the least.

Thank you to my editor, Rebecca: Sometimes it's very hard with all that goes on in my brain to keep my thoughts consistent and clear to the rest of the world. You've done an excellent job of cleaning up my mess. Your contributions were very significant and I am extremely grateful.

To Tariq Nasheed: Thank you for showing me the things I needed to know in order to readjust my life and those who were heavily involved in it. I appreciate every opportunity I've had to tour with you, and I really appreciate you lending your thoughts to this book.

To Mr. Les Brown: When you told me that my style of speaking would reach and revolutionize the world, I was beside myself. I couldn't wrap my mind around the fact that the greatest speaker of any generation would lavish me with such amazing praise! You saw the greatness within me, and you set the bar high enough to challenge my potential. I don't know if I've reached that far yet, but I now believe you and it is my mission to change the world through the greatness that lives in me. Thank you for being an inspiration to me since I was 10 years old! Thank you for your gifts, and your patience. I will never let you down.

To all the friends I've had over the years who are looking for their name right now: Please understand that if I thank each and every one of you who've had an impact on my life, it would take up more pages than the actual book. Rest assured that I acknowledge you. I love you, and your contributions to making me who I am today have not gone unnoticed. This book is my "Thank You" to you. May your days be long, blessed, and filled with an overabundance of love and Common Sense!

-Tazz Daddy

Foreward

There is a new wind breezing through the motivational community who will soon take the world by storm with his unique style and undeniable greatness ... a man who I foresee making an indelible mark on this Earth through his fun, unconventional approach and timeless wisdom. In his new book, Common Sense Ain't Common, Tazz Daddy delivers a comically refreshing perspective on how to recognize and exercise the principles gained through personal experiences. These principles serve as a road map to attaining success.

This book will help you:

- Acquire a broader understanding of how to master the challenges of day to day living,
- Identify patterns of experiences to avoid repetitious cycles that hinder productivity and advancement, and
- Refocus the mindset, expand your skill set, and provide insightful methods that work.

Don't be surprised to find yourself laughing and learning at the same time! Tazz Daddy captivates the reader by attacking the root of why so many people find themselves on the other side of winning. This book will usher you to the next level and catapult your mindset from failure to fulfillment. Tazz Daddy is a name that will soon be known all across the world as a voice of inspiration.

-Les Brown, Motivational Speaker/Speech Coach/ Author

Special Introduction

When presented with advice on life issues, people will oftentimes dismiss it, try to trivialize it, and suspend the use of practicality and Common Sense. We see this every day in news stories or internet blogs spotlighting the lives of celebrities and public figures.

Common Sense would tell certain athletes not to go to a club with a loaded gun ... but they do it anyway. Common Sense would tell certain rappers not to fool around with groupies who are known to write tell all books ... but they do it anyway. Common Sense would tell certain billionaire golfers not to leave voice mails on their side piece's cell phone ... but they do it anyway. These celebrities and other public figures are a microcosm of our society as a whole.

Common Sense will tell people not to smoke crack or crystal meth, but they do it all the time. Thousands of people are addicted to prescription and street drugs despite tons of research and literature documenting that this reckless behavior jeopardizes their mental and physical well-being. Common Sense tells people not to get into relationships with people who have detrimental characteristics. Yet we see it, time and again. Everyday people throw the use of

Common Sense out the window. Many will throw caution to the wind because they have a desire to beat the odds, like living on the edge, and/or want to go against the proverbial grain.

Tazz Daddy has mastered the art of Common Sense, and this book is a great guide to help you do the same.

-Tariq "Elite" Nasheed, New York Times Best-Selling Author, Lecturer, and Entrepreneur

Some Opening Thoughts from Tazz

I've spent the majority of my life as a professional radio broadcaster. I've won several awards, and have succeeded in the highest echelon of my business. That doesn't mean I'm an expert in radio, or an expert in anything really. I am a human being who has learned several valuable lessons. Like others, I have amassed a significant amount of experience over the years. Most of the success I have been fortunate enough to experience can be credited to the good use of Common Sense. Something, you will see, my family made a concerted effort to instill in me.

Chapter 1:
"Common Sense Ain't Common"

According to the dictionary[1], the word *common* means "something belonging to, or shared by all." The word *sense* (the physical senses notwithstanding) is defined as "one's good judgment or realistic point of view." To put it simply, Common Sense is *supposed to be* the good judgment that everyone has. The problem is that everyone doesn't have (or, at the very least, practice) good judgment. It's an oxymoron. It's not common and everyone *clearly* doesn't use it.

The term itself is misleading on many levels. You probably have a great group of friends. I'm speaking about people you can count on for anything. Take a moment and, in your mind's eye, examine the folks at the heart of your group. You've probably shaken your head at one of your friends, maybe more than once, because they didn't exercise Common Sense. There always seems to be one in any given group. If you can't identify the person, then you're very lucky. Or, maybe YOU are "the one." (LOL)

Common Sense is something that you develop over time.

As a child, I can remember being frustrated by stupidity. I'm not saying that I knew everything growing up, but I found that certain things seemed to be more obvious to me than they were to some of my peers.

In elementary school, there was a kid to whom I'll refer as "Rahim." Rahim was smart but, as a 5th grader, seemed more interested in sucking his thumb and being disruptive than he was in learning anything. One day, Rahim ran into the nurse's office leaving a trail of blood and tears in his wake. He had a busted lip and a bloody nose. It looked like he had been attacked by a gang of 8th graders, and that's not an exaggeration. Rahim <u>was</u> attacked - by a slab of asphalt. An attack he provoked and brought on himself. Rahim knew that his shoes were untied. He was told several times before recess. Each time he insisted that he was alright. And he was … until he tripped over his shoelaces and busted his face wide open!

I was very much surprised by my mother's response to the recounting of the day's events. "You've learned a very important lesson today dear," she intoned. I looked up at my mother, partly confused, and partly offended. "Mom," I retorted, "I know better than to run around with my shoes untied. That's Common Sense!" My mother smiled at me and said, "That's my point. Contrary to public opinion and prior belief, Common Sense is NOT a 'given.' As you grow up, people will lead you to believe that everyone is born with the knowledge of how to use Common Sense. This isn't the case."

"Common Sense is like a muscle," my mother continued. "It needs to be conditioned and developed over time. Your experiences in life, and what you take away from them, are what build that muscle. A lot of people make the same mistakes over and over again. Learning from those experiences (so that you don't make the same mistakes again) is the essence of Common Sense." I was lucky; my mother didn't believe in talking to me as if I were a child.

"Rahim knew his shoes were untied, but didn't heed the warnings of others," she said. "You can tell that his parents aren't giving him opportunities to exercise his Common Sense at home, so he doesn't yet know how to use it on his own. It's sad really," she continued. "If he doesn't make some serious changes, he might wind up covering manholes in the street."

While that may seem extreme to some, I've found it to be true. Lack of Common Sense can take you down a path that leaves you poor, lonely, homeless and, worst of all, DEAD. I feel blessed to have a mother who forced me to think critically. I am even luckier that she forced me to learn another key fact: There <u>are</u> consequences for making decisions, both good and bad. So you might as well make good ones.

Life isn't fair & people will lie. Do the right thing anyway.

As a child, most consequences came in the form of a leather belt to my bare ass. Some ass whippings I definitely did not deserve. One of these, the most memorable, came after I was suspended in the eighth grade for helping a kid. "Stuart" was a nerd. In fact, he was a bigger nerd than I was. He was a Jehovah's Witness; and, while there's nothing wrong with that, Stuart made a nasty habit of trying to force his religious beliefs on the rest of the eighth grade class. Some of our classmates got very sick of it and decided to take matters into their own hands.

One unusually boring spring day, we had a substitute math teacher. Not exactly the most titillating topic, his ability to keep our attention was also hindered by a difficult-to-understand African accent. Stuart began talking about Jehovah and Watchtowers, informing all of us that we would be condemned unless we converted to his religion. "Bobby" had enough of Stuart's math class preaching. He and a few others decided to hogtie Stuart, using his own sneaker shoe strings for rope.

The teacher did absolutely nothing to stop this disruption. I asked, "Aren't you going to stop this?" He gave me a very uncomfortable stare and continued trying to teach a math lesson to a classroom that was totally shocked, excited, and appalled by what Bobby was doing to Stuart.

I'm not saying that Bobby acted alone, as there were several boys (and one girl) who got in on the action. I just knew that, as annoying as I found him, Stuart didn't deserve to be hogtied and kicked around. As scared as I was at the thought of that mob turning on me, I protected Stuart and untied him. Would you believe that he wasn't even grateful? "You should've helped me sooner," he scoffed.

Two weeks before 8th grade graduation, we went on a trip to the zoo. Upon our return, ten of us were informed that the Vice-Principal wanted to see us. I thought that we were going to receive some special honor at graduation, but I couldn't have been more wrong. Stuart's mother had marched up to the school and demanded that everyone be expelled! The Vice-Principal only suspended us, but I was outraged!

"I DIDN'T DO ANYTHING BUT HELP HIM," I exclaimed. Unfortunately, all the kids involved in the incident (including Stuart) insisted that I tortured him as well. Later, I discovered that the other kids had received word of what was coming down and they had prepared their story ahead of time. I can only figure that the kids who hogtied Stuart didn't appreciate me getting involved, so this was their way of getting revenge. Stuart thought I didn't act fast enough, so I guess he wanted me to go down as well.

Worse than my "permanent record" having a serious smudge on it, my mother was informed. This meant that she was going to have to take off from work, and brace herself for severe disappointment. The evidence was extremely circumstantial but, since school wasn't a court of law, I was totally screwed.

Getting a spanking was rare, but memories last a lifetime. I am thankful that this was my final one. "Mom," I said, "I didn't do this! All I did was help this idiot. The teacher sat back and did NOTHING! Kids are carrying guns in the school! I do the right thing and I get a spanking?"

My mother said, very matter-of-factly, "The Vice-Principal has no reason to lie. Neither does the substitute teacher. You should be thankful that they are going to let you march at graduation." I was more hurt than anything, because this was the only time in my life that my mother didn't believe me.

My brother, Aaron, was away in college and I called him long-distance to explain the situation. He did a great job of being my own personal Johnnie Cochran, but it was to no avail. The jury was in and I was to be executed by a lethal leather belt. My brother was very frank with me, "Mom will ALWAYS side with the teachers because she's one of them."

After the ass-whipping, a few interesting things happened. I was grounded for the entire summer, which sucked on several levels. Stuart's parents pressed charges on everyone involved in the hogtying incident - except me.

Most importantly, I was given the "Youth Peacemaker of the Year Award" for my work as a youth and family mediator. When I presented these facts to my mother, she told me that there was "a lesson to be learned from this." I told her 3 words: "Believe your son." It was the only time I can recall talking back to my mother without any repercussions.

I learned that doing the right thing didn't always reap rewards. In spite of that, one should always do the right thing - no matter how hard it is. It may cost you some comforts (and possibly some friends), but the reward is worth it. Instilling the habit of good choices will make you a better person in the long run. The truth will find a way to come out. And even if it doesn't, take comfort in standing up for what is right.

Fame and money can't buy Common Sense.

I want to be clear: Common Sense (or a lack thereof) does NOT discriminate. Many people believe that because someone has achieved a certain level of fame or financial security, then they must have an extraordinary level of Common Sense. That isn't always the case.

Tiger Woods, one of the most accomplished and respected golfers in the sport, proved that $1 billion in the bank and all of the fame in the modern world is nothing compared to an ounce of Common Sense. Tiger's lack of Common Sense, and the resulting media frenzy, put him in the spotlight – and not in a pleasant way.

Tiger Woods had been in a car accident. After days of media coverage (and no doubt long hours spent digging into his personal life), we were informed that Tiger's car accident was the result of being chased out of the house by his golf-club-wielding wife. After discovering proof of infidelity via text messages on his cell phone, it's safe to say that she was not pleased. While we don't know all of the details of what happened that night, we do know that Tiger cheated on his wife with at least 18 other women.

First, Tiger Woods should have kept his commitment. And, if that just was not possible (some people seem to be incapable of it), then common sense should have dictated choosing different partners. I'm not advocating cheating. But if he was going to cheat, he should have ensured that the other party had a vested interest. He might as well have loaded cannon, and then set it loose. Common sense should have told him the predicted outcome would not be good. He had everything to lose. His partners had absolutely nothing to lose and everything to gain. When the "secret" got out, every woman who had a questionable interaction with Tiger Woods came forward and collected a nice piece of change and media exposure. Waitresses, restaurant hostesses, porn stars, and strippers do not make for discreet bedfellows - especially if you're a billionaire with one of the most recognizable faces on the entire planet.

Prepare for your role & choose good advisors. Then listen to them.

The resulting media disaster became an even bigger problem for Tiger. And not all of the blame rests solely with him. His advisors, including his father, share some of the responsibility.

As a child, Tiger Woods spent a lot of time with his father on golf courses all across the country. Earl Woods knew that his son was destined for greatness. And, as a black man in a traditionally white sport, his father knew that Tiger would generate a lot of attention. A savvy dad, knowing his son was destined for media attention, would have ensured his son had the skills necessary to live in that world. In spite of this, the only thing his father gave him was a golf club. Given Tiger's behavior, one can assume that his father never talked to him about how to handle fame, women, and sex.

I'm not saying that Tiger should blame his Dad. Just that, as an advisor, his father could have better prepared him. This is true for all of Tiger's advisors. With 18 women involved, it is unreasonable to believe that NONE of his advisors knew what was happening. Just as Michael Jackson's advisors looked the other way when he was abusing prescription medicine, Tiger's advisors looked the other way while he participated in activities potentially dangerous to his career, reputation, and life.

Everybody has issues and skeletons in their closet, ones they hope will never see the light of day. But the playing field is not even, not when you are in the spotlight. Where were his media advisors? Why wasn't he counseled to speak up? Had Tiger Woods been forthright, providing a concise and truthful statement at the very beginning, he could have avoided the majority of the scandal. By not taking a clear stance, he opened the door for the media to take the story and run with it. Every blog site in the world ran at least five or six Tiger Woods stories; and the news media had a field day with him. Both the media speculation and the resulting circus were a direct result of his refusal to take action. Most of the nonsense that Tiger Woods experienced could have easily been prevented. The end result? Tiger Woods lost several endorsements. And his return to golf has been lackluster at best.

It is absolutely paramount that you choose good, knowledgeable people as advisors – and then listen to them. Had either Tiger Woods or Michael Jackson made better choices, the results may have been different. This is especially difficult in their chosen fields. The entertainment industry is filled with self-serving interlopers who profit handsomely off of celebrities while demonstrating very little regard for their well-being. Not wanting to upset the apple cart (or in this case the gravy train), they fail to take action in the best interests of the artist. Unfortunately, one of the biggest problems that entertainers face is that there aren't enough good people to help guide them through the treacherous waters of the industry. Selecting the right advisors is only part of the battle. You need to actually LISTEN to them without letting your ego get in the way.

Don't let an inflated ego get in your way.

When you believe your hype, you tend to have an air of confidence that is based upon an inflated ego. While every person on earth has an ego, an out of control ego can be dangerous. It can lead to making decisions that, had you been thinking rationally, would not otherwise be considered.

Dr. Laura is a prime example of an ego that went unchecked for far too long. In 2010, this nationally syndicated radio personality took to the airwaves and ranted about the use of the N-word in a manner that was totally inappropriate.

Jade, a black woman married to a white man, called in to Dr. Laura's show seeking some practical advice for her marital dilemma. Her husband's friends and family repeatedly made derogatory racial slurs in her presence. They routinely inquired about "The Black Experience." And asked for opinions on how black people react given certain situations. Over time, she began to feel uncomfortable around his white family and friends. At the end of her rope, she wanted some practical advice from a professional. What Jade got was something entirely different.

Jade received a lot of commentary, but none of it answered her question. Instead of hearing what Jade had to say and empathizing with her, Dr. Laura accused Jade of being "hypersensitive." Venting her frustrations about how black people use the N-word, Dr. Laura stated, "If you turn on HBO, you'll hear black comedians say 'Nigger, Nigger, Nigger.'" The commentary continued.

Jade then made a point to tell Dr. Laura that the free usage of the N-word made Jade uncomfortable. Instead of understanding how racially insensitive she was being, Dr. Laura said, "You must not watch HBO."

Regardless of whether or not Jade watches HBO, what black comedians do is nowhere near as offensive as what Dr. Laura did on her program. Saying "nigger" over 11 times is not advisable, especially coming from a counseling professional with a nationally syndicated radio show.

In less than a week, Dr. Laura's show lost 2 major sponsors. Not long after, she appeared on Larry King Live to announce that her last show would be at the end of 2010. This would supposedly allow her to reclaim her First Amendment rights. Had Dr. Laura practiced Common Sense and the slightest bit of self restraint, she would not be forced to leave a nationally syndicated show in disgrace.

I'd like to say that, as an adult, I've exercised Common Sense at every turn. But, if I did, I'd be lying to you. The truth is that, like Rahim, I've fallen on my face and left myself battered and bruised. I can also admit to being hogtied by my bad choices, just like Stuart. The good news is that I've learned from my lack of Common Sense. I contend that learning from my lapses of Common Sense have made me stronger, wiser, and more aware of my place in the universe.

Tazz's Tips: Understanding Common Sense in Practical Terms

- Common Sense is something that you develop over time.
- Life isn't fair & people will lie … do the right thing anyway.
- Fame and money cannot buy Common Sense.
- Prepare for your role & choose good advisors. Then listen to them.
- Don't let an inflated ego get in your way.

"Common Sense is not so common."

  – Voltaire (1694-1778), Writer, Poet, Historian, Philosopher

Chapter 2:
Developing Common Sense

Using "Good Judgment" is essential to developing your Common Sense.

As my mother said, Common Sense is a muscle that needs to be built and exercised. Developing biceps requires weight, repetitions, and proper form. Common Sense requires discipline, repetitions, and Good Judgment. Although NFL Hall of Famer Lawrence Taylor knew a lot about developing his biceps, by not exercising Good Judgment he became another tragic example of what happens when you don't practice Common Sense.

No one will ever know all of the details surrounding Lawrence Taylor's fateful decision to be in a hotel room with an underage prostitute. We can all agree, however, that he should not have been there at all.

Lawrence Taylor had a promising future. He had a beautiful wife, a loving family, and a great post-football career. Somehow, he allowed himself to get caught up in nonsense and his public image was the price he paid. We haven't forgotten Lawrence Taylor's bouts with drugs and alcohol. But, he did such a great job of rehabbing his image, it seemed like he had beaten his demon. Then he allowed an even bigger demon into his life. All of the work he expended fixing one set of bad decisions is now absolutely worthless!

And it didn't have to happen. When you're Lawrence Taylor, you may not get the kind of groupie attention that Terrell Owens would get; but you still do better than our regular Joe coming in off the street. Common Sense should have kicked in and told Lawrence Taylor that he is famous! There is no need to ever deal with a prostitute when you are recognizable. I can safely assume that there will be no more movie roles, television appearances, or broadcasting jobs for Lawrence Taylor in the foreseeable future. He lost all of them because he did not practice Common Sense.

Make a conscious effort to use Common Sense on a regular basis.

Good Judgment and Common Sense are not one time affairs, nor are they autonomic responses. You don't consciously maintain your body temperature. You don't have to think about making your heart beat. It just happens. Not true for Common Sense.

If you want to build stamina, you have to THINK about exercising and make a concerted effort to do so. It's exactly the same with Common Sense. It requires conscious effort to practice.

R&B singer Chris Brown is an example of someone who did not make a conscious effort to practice Common Sense. He allegedly assaulted his girlfriend, Rhianna, after a Grammy party in 2009. Famous or not, a man should never put his hands on a woman at all. As one of the biggest singers of his generation, Chris was making a name for himself. The title of "domestic abuser" was one that he could ill afford.

For months, Chris Brown endured the utter destruction of his public image. His album "Graffiti" flopped. Radio stations stopped playing his singles. Comparing him to the likes of infamous domestic abusers Ike Turner and O.J. Simpson, comedians had a field day making fun of him. At 19 years of age, Chris Brown should have known better.

Chris had not yet learned that Common Sense and Good Judgment require conscious effort and practice. His strange and upsetting television appearances only made matters worse. He appeared inadequate, guilty, and totally unappealing to his fan base. Prior to this incident, Chris had a clean-cut, all-American boy image. Following the incident, video of him playing on a Jet Ski was replaced with images of him in an orange county jump suit picking up trash on the side of the road. Sad and disheartening on many levels, it could have been easily prevented.

Had he made a conscious effort, Good Judgment could have been Chris Brown's best friend. Instead, he chose to make angry rants on twitter and in the media about how unfairly he was treated. Common Sense should have told him that the jury of public opinion had deemed him a woman beater. In the eyes of his fans and detractors, Chris Brown got everything he deserved.

Observe the mistakes of others.

One of the easiest ways to develop your Common Sense is to observe the mistakes of others and consider what you would do differently if you were in their shoes. Hoping to win a big pot, thousands of people buy lottery tickets every single day. Yet, so many lottery winners seem to go broke after winning millions of dollars. The probability is high that a lack of common sense is a deciding factor in every story. Let's take a case in point.

Jack Whittaker ran a contracting firm called Diversified Enterprises Construction. Before he won the lottery, Jack had an estimated net worth of over $1 million. On Christmas Day in 2002, Whittaker went to a convenience store. He bought a sandwich, a tank of gas, and a Powerball Ticket that hit for $315 million. At the time, Whittaker's winnings were the highest lottery payout to an individual in US History. Wisely choosing the lump sum option, he yielded about $113.4 million after taxes. Because Jack Whittaker obviously didn't practice Common Sense, his subsequent decisions after buying that ticket would cause unprecedented havoc in his business, family, and life.

Like most God-fearing Christians, Jack gave 10% of his earnings to his local church. He also started the Jack Whittaker Foundation, a non-profit organization that provides food and clothing to low-income families in his native West Virginia. Additionally, he tipped the woman who worked the convenience store's biscuit counter where he bought the winning ticket. He bought her a $123,000 house, a new Jeep, and gave her $44,000 cash.

Here's where Common Sense could have helped Jack Whittaker. In 2003 Jack's car was parked outside of a strip club called the Pink Pony. Thieves broke in and found $545,000 in cold, hard, cash. No one in their right mind should be stupid enough to leave that kind of money in his car, outside of a strip club, in a town where **EVERYONE** knows you've just won the lottery. But Jack Whittaker was long on cash and obviously short on Common Sense.

Did he learn from his mistake? No. In January 2004, thieves again broke into his car and stole over $200,000 in cash. This cash was later recovered.

Not long after the second robbery, Whittaker was

arrested for allegedly threatening the life of a bar manager. He settled out of court for an undisclosed amount of money. A couple of months later, a woman sued Jack Whittaker for allegedly groping her at a dog racetrack. Again, he settled out of court for an undisclosed amount of money. When he was asked about the legal troubles that had befallen him, Whittaker smugly replied, "It doesn't bother me because I can tell everyone to kiss off!"

The aforementioned lawsuits ruined Jack Whittaker financially. He also lost family, friends, and most importantly his privacy and self-respect. Even the biggest US lottery payout wasn't enough to save Jack Whittaker from a deficiency of Common Sense.

"Common Sense Ain't Common" isn't just the title of this book; it is a very real fact of life. If you choose not to use it, you'll become a victim of crimes that you commit against yourself.

Tazz's Tips: Developing Common Sense

- Using "Good Judgment" is essential to developing your Common Sense.
- Make a conscious effort to use Common Sense on a regular basis.
- Observe the mistakes of others.

"Common sense is in spite of, not as the result of, education."

-Victor Hugo (1802–1885) Poet, Statesman, Human Rights Activist

Chapter 3:
The Limits We Place On Ourselves

Man has created marvelous wonders and achievements. When I walk the streets of my native Philadelphia, I'm blown away by the buildings that make up the skyline. I'm moved by the ingenuity it must have taken to build the pyramids of Egypt, without computers or modern machinery. And no matter how many times I've experienced it, safely taking off and landing in a jumbo jet is utterly amazing.

While mankind is capable of incredible creations, we can destroy with the same amount of creativity and precision. Evidence of this is abundant. The nuclear arms race of the 1980's, the BP oil spill of 2010, and the Iraq War are all prime examples. Whether it's creation or destruction, mankind has been able to do "the impossible."

We are only limited by what we can "see." Vision is one of the main things that dictate our success and happiness and life. The dictionary[2] defines *vision* as "a mental image of something that is imaginary." Even the word *imagine* comes from the word *image*! Do you remember the power that you could unleash by using your imagination?

Forget being "realistic"! Your imagination is the key to unlocking your potential success.

When I was a kid, my imagination could turn two ordinary cardboard boxes into an impenetrable fortress, complete with a lookout tower and gun turrets (old broomsticks). As I approached adolescence, I rushed home to sketch and document all the fully developed comic book characters and short stories that my imagination created. It seemed as though they just came pouring out of my brain. What happens to us when we reach adulthood? In my opinion, society happens. The pressure to be considered "normal" and accepted by people (who don't matter at all) happens. Pressure can be overwhelming, but only if you allow it to be. No one ever wants to be the odd-man-out; but, in order to be exceptional, you're going to have to be.

Learn how to dream and imagine again. It doesn't require much, just a desire to reconnect with your positive immaturity. Whenever anyone begins to take on a childlike outlook on daily life, so-called "mature" people will quickly tell that person to "grow up." If you let the "Grow Up" mentality set into your life, it will stunt your growth. Ironic, isn't it? Look at Peter Pan: A boy who never grew up! A boy who fought PIRATES for fun! WITHOUT FEAR! A boy who could fly just by thinking happy thoughts! A naysayer would say *"Peter Pan wasn't real, and even if he was, it was Tinkerbell's fairy dust that gave him the ability to fly."* They would be wrong! While Tinkerbell did supply Peter Pan with fairy dust, it would have been useless to him if he didn't have a happy thought and the ability to focus on it relentlessly.

Without having a clear vision and the willingness to see it through, your dreams won't come true. Sometimes that means that your vision may seem impossible to others; but that's because those who lack vision need to have something they can see in order to believe. Don't focus on them. Rather, focus on creating something that everyone can see.

Let's pretend for a moment that, ever since you were a child, you've had a dream of owning a Hair Salon. Nothing makes you happier than making people look their best. You went to beauty school, graduated with flying colors, and obtained a great job at a reputable salon. While most people would throw themselves a tickertape parade at this point, you're not satisfied. That little kid is staring back at you in the mirror, reminding you of a self-made promise so many years ago. It is at this moment the *real* battle begins: the fight you start with yourself.

Before I go any further with our imaginary hair salon example, let me address those of you who think that's crazy – or who think I'm crazy. While several people I know may agree with your assessment, it doesn't make what I'm telling you any less valid. Internal conflict is **REAL.** It kills millions of goals and dreams on a daily basis. Here's what happens: You want to pursue your true purpose in life, but the closer you get to making things happen, the more you begin to doubt yourself. Self doubt is what keeps runners from winning races, keeps men from asking that gorgeous girl on a date, and keeps some businesspeople from asking their bosses for a raise they know they deserve. Self doubt is a crippling force, yet we never discuss it. It continues to infect us, one by one.

The human soul is like a sponge, soaking up whatever it touches. Without knowing you personally, I can assume that you've come in contact with a naysayer or two in your life. A lot of these people say they want to "save you from disappointment." The rest are people who can't do what you're about to accomplish. Even if you're extremely positive, years of those influences have planted seeds of doubt in your spirit.

The only thing that stands between you and success is You. Defeat the Doubt Monster!

Let's continue with our imaginary hair salon example, shall we? When you embark on the journey toward owning your salon, those dormant seeds of doubt grow into a monstrous version of yourself. One that is part attorney, part Freddy Krueger. I call this creature of our subconscious "The Doubt Monster." The Doubt Monster will lay the smackdown on your dreams by using the deadliest weapon known to man: Logic. You, armed with your belief, will do battle in a back-and-forth that only ends when, defeated, one of you gives in. The Doubt Monster will always let you start the debate. Let's listen in on the conversation.

You	I can open a salon and be successful.
Doubt Monster	*(retorts)* The majority of businesses will fail within their first year!
You	I've got a great clientele and an eye for other talented stylists! I could probably hire a phenomenal staff and be tremendously successful!
Doubt Monster	*(without batting an eye)* You and every other hairstylist think they will take over the world. In actuality, you're not very spectacular. Your credit isn't that good, so getting a loan for a building is out of the question. You don't have a marketing budget to advertise, so you'll just be another hair salon in the

phonebook, along with the thousands
of others. How do you think you can
possibly pull this off?

At this point, you have two choices. You can listen to the
practicality and sobering logic of the Doubt Monster, or you
can spit directly in logic's face and MAKE IT HAPPEN.
I want to be clear. I'm not saying that you can simply snap
your fingers and everything will somehow magically fall
into place. I'm saying that your hard work, preparation,
and determination make the "Fairy Dust." Your dreams,
goals, and aspirations are your "Happy Thoughts." The
combination, along with relentless focus, will allow you to
fly. One part without the other is absolutely useless.

HOW is not your problem.

I'm fairly certain that some of you are thinking: *"Tazz,
how can I ever get my dreams to become my reality?"* My
good friend, Les Brown, says it best: *"HOW* is not your
problem." Simply put, if you move towards your goals with
a sincere and deliberate effort, opportunities and resources
will reveal themselves to you. Proverbs 18:16 says, "A man's
gift makes room for him and brings him before great men."
In other words, God has given you everything you need to
be successful, all you have to do is put those gifts to good
use.

Become your own Trailblazer.

Don't be afraid of being the first person to do something. Lab
rats follow a path that someone created *for* them. You're not

a lab rat, you're a human being. You're capable of so much more. I encourage you to act like it. Instead of following along the safe path, BE the greatness that you want in your life! I'm challenging you to do more than choose your own path; I'm daring you to blaze a trail! Just because something hasn't been done before, doesn't mean that you can't be the first person to bring it to life!

For many years, mainstream media and sports authorities perpetuated the idea that it was physically impossible for human beings to run a mile in under four minutes. This "fact" held true until a man named Roger Bannister broke the four minute mile barrier in 1954. After Bannister broke the record, several people across the world were running a mile in less than four minutes. Remember when I told you that those who lack vision need to have something they can see in order to believe? This is a prime example. Once the four minute mile barrier was broken, another barrier was broken: the barrier of impossibility. Breaking the barrier of impossibility takes more than just belief, it also takes determination.

Stick with it.

Roger Bannister finished in fifth place to qualify for the 1952 Olympics. What's even more interesting is that he came in fourth place in his Olympic event. To put it another way, he trained, ate all of the right things, and only wound up in fourth place. This means that Roger Bannister committed a tremendous amount of his life to being a winner in the Olympic Games, and he didn't succeed.

For two months after Roger Bannister's disappointing Olympic performance, The Doubt Monster went to work on his self-esteem. Surprisingly enough, The Doubt Monster almost won. Bannister was almost convinced to give up running. Imagine if he had given up. Bannister would have missed his place in history! Had Bannister given up on running, we may have waited a long time until the four minute mile was ever broken, maybe until Carl Lewis or Usain Bolt.

When you're working on your dreams, there is more at stake than how they affect you. Your dreams, goals or aspirations may inspire someone in the future to achieve new heights. Roger Bannister is just one example of how moving forward can impact the world. If you doubt me, ask yourself if anyone talks about the runners who received medals in Bannister's Olympic event.

Your destiny is bigger than your dreams.

Tazz's Tips: Removing Limits

- Forget being "realistic"! Your imagination is the key to unlocking your potential success.
- The only thing that stands between you and success is You. Defeat the Doubt Monster!
- HOW is not your problem.
- Become your own Trailblazer.
- Stick with it.

"Being realistic is the most commonly traveled road to mediocrity."

- Will Smith (1968–), Actor, Rapper, Producer

Chapter 4:
Reach Your Vision

Science, Art, Sports ... every field has its masters. Their common thread is a fully formed vision, focused action, and a positive attitude.

Find a way to overcome Procrastination.

Most people don't know that the great Leonardo DaVinci was a natural procrastinator. He was known to doodle and daydream. And, he almost NEVER FINISHED A PROJECT ON TIME! DaVinci, like most popular artists of his time, had sponsors who were commonly called "Patrons." *The Last Supper* was finally completed because DaVinci's patron threatened to cut him off financially. The *Mona Lisa* took twenty years to complete.

And beyond his procrastination, he had his own Doubt Monster with whom to contend. This genius who totally changed the face of art, engineering, architecture, biology, botany, anatomy, math, and physics wondered about his contributions. It is rumored that DaVinci appealed to God by saying, "Tell me if anything was done."

I'm not God, but I can safely say that DaVinci accomplished a great deal.

- He created plans for flying machines that, 600 years later, would be the basis for helicopters and airplanes.
- He developed the prototype for what would become a submarine.
- He designed an armored vehicle which is the basis for the modern tank.
- His *Vitruvian Man* is considered a cultural icon.
- Most people would agree that the *Mona Lisa* and *The Last Supper* are two of the most recognizable pieces of art on Earth!

DaVinci overcame procrastination because he had a motivating force – his patrons. My motivating force is ensuring that I make an impact on the world. Figure out what motivates you, and then leverage it to reach your ultimate potential.

See past the temporary limitations of your current circumstances.

When I hear people whine about their upbringing, using it as an excuse for a life in shambles, I think of DaVinci. DaVinci was the illegitimate son of a Notary and a peasant woman. In other words, by virtue of birth, DaVinci was not accepted into high society.

I know people who are the products of teenage mothers, one night stands, or a busted condom. These people feel that the circumstances surrounding their birth are somehow an indicator for how their lives will turn out. Nothing could be further from the truth. DaVinci's father didn't have a "legitimate" child until Leonardo was around 16. Without using Google or Wikipedia, I challenge you to tell me his name. I'm willing to bet that you can't.

Despite his problems with procrastination and social standing, Leonardo DaVinci changed the world forever. So what if your Daddy was never there? So what if your Momma was a prostitute? So what you came from the hood and no one before you has ever made it out? Those are all other people's choices, NOT YOURS! Any circumstance in your life can be changed, as long as you are willing to change it!

If you were to get caught in the rain without an umbrella and wound up soaking wet, would you decide to never venture out again? I certainly hope not. Common Sense should kick in and tell you to keep a small umbrella with you.

Other people's actions can have an effect on you, but only if you allow it. When you were a child, you had no control over your environment and the way you were raised. This is not true as an adult. You have a lot of control over your environment. Further, as an adult, you are totally responsible for how you see the world. You can create a positive environment for yourself, including your attitude. Or you can choose to be a victim. The bills come in your name, so why squander time whining about what other people have/haven't done to or for you? It's a true waste of your time and a massive hindrance when it comes to achieving your greatness.

Some of you are probably wondering, "So, Tazz, you said that other people's actions can have an effect on me, but only if I allow it. What exactly does that mean? What do I do about that?" I'm glad you asked! Control your environment! Including the people with whom you associate.

A "woe is me" attitude can actually infect you.

As a matter of self-preservation, I've had to eliminate several people from my life because they were limiting my ability to take steps towards greatness. It's not that they were bad people, but their energy was toxic. Those with a "woe is me" attitude can actually infect you, should you allow it.

In my case, I tried to help my former friends see that their circumstances could change if only they changed their perspective. When I realized that my words were falling upon deaf ears, I moved on. I refuse to be around toxic people who make a conscious decision to remain that way. If that sounds a little cold to you, it is. There is no excuse for purposely being a toxic person. I should know; I used to be toxic. When bad things happened to me, I blamed anything and everything, everyone and anyone, until I realized one very important fact: Blaming doesn't change your circumstances. Complaining doesn't eliminate your problems. No one wants to help a complainer, and no one accepts excuses.

Accept no excuses.

There is never an excuse for not achieving your greatness. Physical, environmental, and financial limitations can all be overcome. Helen Keller was blind and deaf, and yet she never let it stop her from writing books, giving lectures and becoming a political activist. A lot of people won't get up off the couch to pursue their dreams and they have perfect hearing and sight. These people have been blinded by the fear of failure and have been deafened by doubt. Failure is an illusion. The only true failure is not learning from one's mistakes.

Helen Keller once said, "There's no king who has not had a slave among his ancestors, and no slave who has not had a king among his." I can't say for sure what she meant when she said it, but I take it to mean that anyone is capable of greatness ... or living a generic life.

Do not allow yourself to make excuses. There are no limits to the greatness that you can achieve. There is no magical predetermination as to who becomes great. It's as simple as having a vision, making a plan, and working toward it. You must not let anything stop you, including The Doubt Monster.

Have a clear vision, and the willingness to see it through, no matter what!

Michael Jordan is regarded by many sports enthusiasts as the greatest player to have ever picked up a basketball. And yet, he was cut from his high school basketball team. Michael Jordan did not let that stop him from becoming one of the greatest basketball players in the history of the world. Instead, he practiced, worked hard, and developed his skills until he made the team. He dominated the sport in college, and was drafted to the Chicago Bulls. The rest, as they say, is history. Like Dr. J and Wilt Chamberlain before him, Michael Jordan was regarded by his peers and millions of people across the world as a man who changed the face of professional sports forever. I think it's safe to say that the players on his high school basketball team don't hold that distinction. Sometimes it's important to realize that hard work, a positive attitude, and sheer unadulterated determination can take you farther in life than talent alone ever could.

Don't acknowledge limits – work hard to reach your goal.

The mainstream media and society would lead you to believe that it's either amazing talent or dumb luck that leads to success. Nothing could be further from the truth. There are those who get a meteoric rise to fame, but it rarely stands the test of time. That's a "fool's gold" version of success. Michael Jordan practiced before the team practice began and after the team practice was over. That is the kind of dedication and determination that spawns greatness.

There are people who may not be as smart as you. There are people who may not be as gifted as you. If any of the aforementioned people decide to outwork you, they WILL be more successful than you. Those people don't acknowledge their limits; they work hard and deliberately towards their dreams. That's exactly what you should do!

Forget about the sky being the limit! Live in a universe where limits don't exist! It's at that moment that the success of which you've been dreaming will be given to you.

Tazz's Tips: Reaching Your Vision

- Find a way to overcome Procrastination
- See past the temporary limitations of your current circumstances.
- A "woe is me" attitude can actually infect you.
- Accept no excuses.

- Have a clear vision, and the willingness to see it through, no matter what!
- Don't acknowledge limits - work hard to reach your goal.

"Leaders are visionaries with a poorly developed sense of fear and no concept of the odds against them. They make the impossible happen."

-Dr. Robert Jarvik (1946-), Designer & Biomedical Engineer, Inventor of the first permanently-implantable artificial heart.

Chapter 5: Accidents Don't Happen ... They Are Caused

Avoid accidents by making good choices.

Ever have your parents tell you not to play ball in the house? Remember the statement that always followed? You'll break something. Like most 10 year old boys, I heard that a lot. Did I listen? No. I learned that lesson that hard way. I can still see it in slow motion, the ball, the impact, my mother's favorite lamp falling before I could reach it, and the terrible sound of it breaking apart. Staring at the shattered porcelain, I came to the unsettling realization that my ass was grass and Edythe was the lawnmower.

I sat on the edge of the couch, dreadfully awaiting my mother's impending arrival. When she finally arrived, it only took one glance. The picture I made, sitting there with my head in my hands next to a conspicuously empty end table, pretty much told the story. After explaining, I admitted that I had no business playing in the house. I also told her how sorry I was and that it was an accident. I was both paralyzed with fear and severely disappointed in myself for hurting my mother. Tears already streaming down my face, I braced for impact.

Instead of tanning my hide immediately, my mother went upstairs, put on some comfortable clothes, and returned to the living room. I still couldn't look her in the eyes. She sat down next to me, lifted my head and said, "Look at me." Reluctantly, I opened my eyes and faced her. My mother must have taken pity on me because she wiped my tears and made me blow my nose before she began to deliver my punishment.

"Accidents don't happen, they are caused," she stated. At this moment I defended myself as if my life depended on it. "Mom," I implored, "I swear I would've never broken your lamp on purpose. I didn't mean to! It was an accident!" My mother, more amused than she was angry, began to clarify her statement so that I could understand. "Honey," she said, "If you weren't playing ball in the house, the lamp wouldn't have been broken. People use the word 'accident' to absolve themselves of personal responsibility. You didn't intend to break the lamp, but you still caused it to break."

For some reason, my mother took pity on me and mercifully docked my allowance until I paid off the cost of replacing the lamp. I guess she decided that I had punished myself enough. She didn't see a reason to compound the pain I felt in my heart with a spanking. While writing this book, I reminded my mother about this very incident. Neither of us remembered what the lamp looked like, or if it was ever replaced. I do, however, remember the lesson. And that, my friends, is much more important to my mother.

The dictionary[3] defines the word *accident* as "an unexpected event, especially one resulting in damage." Some of its synonyms are *calamity, casualty, disaster,* and *hazard.*

Its antonyms are *intent, necessity, plan,* and *provision.* Wow! Even after having learned the lesson, I had to take a moment to process that! It's like my mother said, it doesn't matter whether I intended to break the lamp or not, damage was caused. All accidents are unnecessary and can be prevented by careful planning and preparation. A corollary to that rule is that there are no "accidental victims."

Decide to take control of your life!

I've encountered several people throughout the course of my life who are perpetual victims (more commonly referred to as "losers"). These people whine and complain about every little difficulty that comes their way in life. It's a sickness! I'm not a psychologist, but Common Sense tells me that nothing good can come from being a perpetual victim.

Here's what I know: Life ISN'T fair. Problems occur in everyone's life. We all have moments of anger, sadness, depression, love, hate, and lust. No human being is better than another and we're all the same in God's eyes. If we all go through the same things, it is our <u>response</u> to these things that determines how we come out of our circumstances.

When you look at your life as one big accident, you have no control over anything. You're as strong as a leaf in the wind. You're going where life decides to take you. No one with all of their mental faculties should live that way, but millions of people do. These people lack a strong foundation and suffer from misdirection. These perpetual victims are people who *allow* life to happen to them. Most of them have little to no intent, no plan, and have made no provisions to fulfill their purpose.

Sadly, most perpetual victims will waste their time telling you that they have it all together. They will dismiss the notion that they are living a loser's existence. There are many reasons why people find themselves in that horrible state, but the reasons are unimportant. You may be thinking, "If the reasons aren't important, then exactly what part of this IS important?" I'm glad you asked. The important part is the method by which they escape this fate. "And, how does one go about doing that, Tazz?" Good question! The method is simple: Develop a winner's mindset.

Winners achieve greatness by deliberate action. Make moves; don't just talk about making moves!

People believe that winners have it all together. Nothing could be further from the truth. Nevertheless, the winner's mindset is self assured, regardless of what is going on around them. A winner has a plan and will do whatever it takes (on the right side of the law) to make it happen.

Winners do not become winners by accident, they become winners by ACTION. Everything a winner does is extremely calculated and deliberate. They make it their business to see the finish line at the start of the race. Winners do not acknowledge competition, because they are only competing with their previous accomplishments and achievements. Winners are like race horses; they have blinders on, and they move forward with relentless aggression and determination.

Am I feeding you a healthy diet of moonbeams and starlight? Absolutely not! I'm not telling you that winners do not experience problems, because that would be utterly ridiculous. It is my contention that winners experience more problems in their quest for greatness than do perpetual victims who pursue nothing tangible. Regardless of which group encounters the higher number of problems, their philosophies in handling these obstacles are as different as night and day. Winners respond to problems, while perpetual victims complain about them.

Have you ever noticed that people who live their lives as perpetual victims keep trying the same thing, the same way, while expecting different results? That, according to Albert Einstein, is the definition of insanity. Perpetual victims specialize in a special form of insanity; the kind that causes them to lose more and more self esteem with every failure.

People with a winner's mindset understand and accept that failure is a probability along the way; they don't let that deter them from their goals. More importantly, winners never take failure personally, they learn from it. To winners, every failure is an opportunity from which to learn.

Walt Disney is quoted as saying, "All our dreams can come true, if we have the courage to pursue them." He would know. His dream to open an amusement park was not an easy road. He was turned down multiple times for a bank loan. Although Walt may be the only one who knows the exact number, references can be found to being turned down 60+, 80+, 300+ and 500+ times. Think about it. Even if the smallest number were correct, he was turned down more than 60 times! Did he call himself a failure and give up? No! And you shouldn't either.

Winners know how to separate themselves from their failures. After all, if they believed that they were failures, they would never succeed. Their mindset isn't accidental; and neither are their results.

Your existence is not an accident! Your life is a series of choices.

Trial and error are necessary for ultimate success. Perpetual victims live to sing their song of woe to whoever will listen. Someone told me once, "I might as well kill myself! My whole life is one big accident! Even my birth wasn't planned!" I looked at him and said, "Let me prove you wrong."

"Accidents don't happen they are caused!" I said. "Even if your mother was pregnant with you on purpose, your father released up to 600 million sperm. Out of all of those sperm, only one reached the egg that created the embryo that turned into you. As the sperm travels into the cervix towards the egg, it comes to a crossroad. It must guess which fallopian tube contains the egg. Even if it chooses the right one, that sperm is not alone. There are hundreds of thousands of sperm trying to penetrate that one egg. Whichever sperm penetrates the egg first, succeeds in fertilizing it. The other 599,999,999 sperm die off. You didn't happen by accident! Your existence was a series of choices, the most important of which took place after your parents had sex. So there was no mistake or accident that you are here instead of someone else. You won a huge race just to have the privilege of living, so why would you think of yourself as anything less than the winner that you are?"

My friend looked at me, shocked by my perspective. After a moment he simply said, "I appreciate you, and I know what I need to do." From there, he enrolled in school and now has a very successful entertainment business. I am not taking credit turning for his life around, but I know it didn't happen by accident!

How did my friend turn things around? He was still facing the same adversity; that hadn't changed. The only thing different was his attitude. He CHOSE a different reaction, and then he committed to it.

Tazz's Tips: Preventing Accidents

- Avoid accidents by making good choices.
- Decide to take control of your life!
- Winners achieve greatness by deliberate action. Make moves; don't just talk about making moves!
- Your existence is not an accident! Your life is a series of choices.

"I don't believe in accidents. There are only encounters in history. There are no accidents."

-Elie Wiesel (1928-), Nobel Laureate, Winner of the Presidential Medal of Freedom, Winner of the Congressional Gold Medal

Chapter 6:
Obstacles Only Have the Power You Give Them

Do you feel as if there is some daunting, impossible task or obstacle that will ultimately keep you from achieving your goals? This thought process goes beyond The Doubt Monster. The Doubt Monster operates by telling you what obstacles <u>could</u> appear. Choosing to feel as if there is an insurmountable obstacle before it even appears is crazy! You're admitting defeat before you start.

Now let's take a look at how you operate when confronted with an actual obstacle. Obstacles will appear, that's a given. But very, very few are insurmountable. The truth is: There is no force on Earth that can stop you without your help.

Obstacles are only temporary. Find a way to make them a memory!

One of my favorite books talks about the unimportance of obstacles. It says that if you have faith the size of a mustard seed, you can point to a mountain, tell it to move and it will obey you. It may sound like a bunch of mythical crap, but it's Common Sense. My father watched me get frustrated over some project, and his stern but loving voice put things in perspective. "Boy, don't make a mountain out of a mole hill." He told me to take my time and figure out a way to accomplish my goals. With my parents, giving up because of an obstacle wasn't even an option.

My father used to tell me, "Trouble South? Go North. Trouble East? Go West." In layman's terms what I think my father was trying to tell me was that sometimes the best way to deal with an obstacle is to maneuver around it, find another way. I also took it to mean that sometimes the best way to deal with an obstacle is to avoid it altogether.

I don't know what obstacles you are facing in your life, but I do know that they are temporary. You just have to find a way to make them a memory. Think about the biggest obstacle you faced five years ago. Can you remember it? I'm willing to bet that you can't. Even if you can, is it still in issue now? I'm guessing it's no longer relevant.

It's not what you go through; it's how you react to what you go through!

My dad was a man's man. He never complained; and if he did, I never heard about it. (My mother may beg to differ.) I know that he never let anything stop him. My great uncle, Sam, nicknamed him "Rock" because, when my father had his mind made up about something, he could not be moved. Adversity had about as much effect on Carl Anderson as water does on a duck's back. Even one of the toughest adversaries he ever faced, the ghost of another person's painful memories, was no match for my father.

In my mother's day, she put models to shame. A gorgeous statuesque woman, she had long hair, cinnamon skin, and a beautiful smile. According to my father she was the original MILF. After going through a harrowing ordeal with her first husband, my mother's patience and trust in men was in short supply. Making matters worse, my mother had recently broken up with a professional football player - after learning about his wife!

The night my father met my mother, she was not in the best frame of mind for such things. My father watched as Mom told one man after another to take a hike. She blew everyone off. He sat back, observed, and watched the carnage. Did that stop him? No. He approached my mother in spite of everyone else's failure. My father didn't hesitate for a second. After spending several minutes admiring the view, my father made his move. He and my mother talked, danced the night away, and exchanged numbers that night. They were married two years later. My father didn't get into doubt, his insecurities, or anything else. He was a man on a mission, and I am living proof that he accomplished his goal!

My parent's love affair is an example of what happens when we fixate on the goal and seize the opportunity. Sometimes we stop due to perceived adversity. This is toxic behavior, because it kills your dreams. Sadly, this toxicity is self-inflicted. Especially when the perceived adversity is an obstacle you created or left in the way.

Remove obstacles.

My nine-year-old nephew, AJ, and his big sister, Kiarra, share a scooter, one that resembles a skateboard. AJ has a habit of leaving the scooter right at the front door. "AJ,"

I said, "don't leave the scooter in the doorway! Someone could break their neck." Without missing a beat, my nephew retorted, "Why wouldn't they just move it out of the way? It's not like they can't see it." I truly believe that my nephew wasn't being disrespectful; he was simply giving an innocent nine-year-old's perspective on life.

This is the key … something you innocently see as "something to watch for" might be something that someone else stumbles over. Or, you might stumble over it yourself! Take preventative action. Don't leave the scooter in the middle of the way – yours or anyone else's.

Get out of your own way!

As sure as you're reading this, your life will be filled with obstacles. In order to succeed you must get over yourself. That's right! I'm saying that the obstacles aren't the issue, YOU are! More specifically, the power you give the obstacle is the issue. The dictionary[4] defines *obstacle* as "something that is in the way." That's it. No fancy, scary language. No message of impending doom, just something that is in the way. If we believe the dictionary, then we must accept that it is the spirit of fear infused with negative energy that gives an obstacle its power.

Be Fearless.

The older we get, the more we seem to get bogged down in the trials and tribulations of life. However, children tend to be fearless, unaware of what an obstacle is. Think about your own childhood for moment. If it's anything like mine, I'm sure it was full of unnecessary risks. I tried to reach the highest branches when I climbed a tree. When it came to bicycling or skateboarding, knee pads and helmets were for sissies. Scraped knees and scars were badges of honor. There wasn't a tree I wouldn't climb or train tracks that wouldn't be explored. Was this behavior responsible? No. But we develop that "Devil May Care" attitude for a reason. We need it to face down obstacles.

The Doubt Monster and an "adult worldview" have combined forces to create fear, as well as make people weak and insecure. This is a huge factor that keeps you from success. In that mindset, a piece of paper in the doorway might as well be a castle, protected by a fire breathing dragon and soldiers brandishing bows and arrows. Fear will paralyze you, keeping you from making the first step in moving even something as insubstantial as paper out of your way. When you add fear to any situation, especially one that has an obstacle, it is you and your fear that hold you back, not the obstacle.

If you can't be fearless, use fear to your advantage!

As a child I spent my summers with my father in Harrisburg, Pennsylvania. In comparison to the bright lights of the city of Philadelphia, it's kind of a slow town with not much to do. At least that's how I saw it. In my neighborhood there was a boy named "Todd." Todd didn't like me very much because I was black. I know this because he told me, "I don't like you because you're black."

Todd was much bigger than I was. And, to be perfectly honest, I was afraid of him. One day, while riding my bike through the neighborhood, Todd placed himself directly in front of my path. He took my bike from me and told me he

47

was not going to give it back. Scared and devastated, I ran home with tears streaming down my face.

As I explained what happened, I could see the concern and anger behind my father's eyes. He wiped my tears, gave me something to drink, and instructed me to come with him. Without hesitation, my father marched me right down to Todd's house and forced me to ring the doorbell. While I was a short, chubby kid, my father was a mountain of a man. Several years of law enforcement perfected his intimidating stare. Todd's father answered the door; and when he saw my father, he damn near crapped his pants!

My father never lost eye contact with Todd's father. His speech was very steady as he said to me, "Tell Todd's father what happened." As I briefly laid out the story for Todd's father, I could see the fear and embarrassment overtake him all at once. He excused himself for a brief moment, grabbed Todd (who just rode up on my bike), and forced him to apologize. Taking possession of my bike, my father looked at Todd and then turned his attention to his father. "I don't take kindly to racists or bullies. The next time my son has a problem with Todd, all bets are off!"

As we walked home, my father informed me that if Todd ever tried to take anything of mine again, I was to "beat him like he stole something." I explained that I was scared and didn't think it was possible to ever beat Todd. My father gave me my first lesson in ultimatums. He said, "Do you want to have to fight Todd? or me?" Immediately, I knew exactly what he meant. If I was going to let anyone intimidate me, my punishment would be to fight the one man with whom no one ever wanted a problem. Needless to say, I never had another problem with a bully again. That was a defining moment for me.

If you really want the best out of your life, you cannot let obstacles stop you. You must get past the fear of the obstacle, and replace it with the fear of not having fulfilled your purpose on Earth before dying. You are the catalyst. You are the hero for whom you've been looking. You are the one to unlock your potential. You are the one to make all of your dreams come true. Get out of your own way! Do not back down! Do not settle for less! Know your value! Understand your mission, and move forward with a purpose that is undeniable. People will respect and admire your newfound confidence. Right now, make a vow to yourself. Vow that there is no man, beast, or anything else that will stop you from achieving your goals. This is your time! Face your obstacles head-on, and move them out of your way!

Tazz's Tips: Dealing with Obstacles

- Obstacles are only temporary. Find a way to make them a memory!
- It's not what you go through; it's how you react to what you go through!
- Remove obstacles.
- Get out of your own way!
- Be Fearless.
- If you can't be fearless, use fear to your advantage!

"We must overcome the notion that we must be regular ... it robs you of the chance to be extraordinary and leads you to the mediocre."

   -Uta Hagen (1919-2004), Tony Award winning Actress, Author, Drama Teacher

Chapter 7:
Friends and Haters

No one person is totally your friend or is totally a hater.

Throughout this book, I have given definitions to all the major words that I've discussed. The terms *friend* and *hate*r, however, are totally up to an individual's personal interpretation.

Most people would contend that a friend is supposed to make you feel good. A friend is supposed to be there when you're up, and should be there for you when you're down. A friend should be a supporter, an ear to lean on, and someone who is there for you no matter what circumstance comes your way. A friend should not be judgmental of you; he should always hold your best interests as a top priority.

A hater is a tricky thing. The term has been used so loosely that it has almost become a cliché. You can hear people talking about haters in songs, on twitter, behind the counter at a fast food restaurant, or in the gleaming high-rise buildings of corporate America. The Hater Phenomenon has become a global brand. One that is very useless in most cases, and often unfounded. Haters never want you to succeed. It is a hater's mission to try to stop your success at every turn. If that's not possible, then a hater must take time out of his or her busy schedule to talk badly about you to whoever will listen. Haters mean you no Earthly good. With every single thing you attempt, they pray earnestly for your downfall. Being a hater is a full-time job with absolutely crappy benefits.

It is my belief that no one person is totally your friend or is totally a hater. I believe that most people live in a gray area. If we are lucky, we may experience two to five true friends in our entire lives! These are people who have been there for us through thick and thin, and wouldn't hesitate to be there again should the need arise. Friends are true treasures and, as such, they should be valued above all others. Their opinions should be respected, even when we don't agree with what they have to say. Some of our friends may find it difficult to deal with us on a consistent basis. Regardless, they will always be there for us when we need them the most. Conversely, haters will be there when we need them the least.

Understand the on-line communication barrier. Don't assume – ask.

Modern society seems to be basically lived and operated on the internet. We no longer send letters to each other; we send e-mails. Many people don't even like to talk to each other on the phone, so they text each other instead. A few years ago, many deaths were attributed to drinking and driving.

Now the news is filled with how many texting and driving related accidents are causing harm to unsuspecting victims. When I was a kid, all of my friends and I would gather at the local arcade in the mall to play video games. Nowadays, all we have to do is turn on the Xbox and play with friends over the internet. We have become a virtual society where face-to-face interaction is a rarity. Between all of the e-mails, the poking, the texts, and the tweets, we're prisoners of a society that has all of the interactions, but none of the human subtleties. That is a big part of our human dilemma right now.

After reading this, you have no idea how my inflection may have changed the meaning of my words. How many times have you read a text message or an e-mail that angered you? How many times has that e-mail been misconstrued? I'm willing to guess it's happened several times in your life. If you couple that with how sensitive and politically correct everyone has become, you have a recipe for utter disaster. I have seen many friendships come to an end over a misunderstanding that took place on the internet. What if these people had understood the on-line communication barrier? What if, instead of assuming what was meant, they asked?

Know when to "Get Out" – and do it early!

"Darron Cheshire" was a very popular entertainer who made the jump to radio comedian, but never mastered the craft of being a real radio personality. When corporate pressured Darron to conform in a more traditional manner, he didn't know how to act. He let his insecurities, pride, and paranoia get the better of him. Darron earned a reputation of being "very difficult to work with." He lashed out often;

or, conversely, he shut down and became distant from both the cast and management.

I could see his potential, so I tried to guide him. When that didn't work, I tried something else. But Darron wasn't listening. And, truth be told, I didn't listen to him either. Darron's behavior made it clear that he was completely uninterested in making any changes. And yet, I kept trying. Not only did this behavior continue, it escalated. When Darron was angry about something (usually something that had been misconstrued or taken out of context), he made hate-filled on-air rants. Some of these rants became an issue for affiliates (individual cities that carried the show), and they raised concerns with corporate. Corporate couldn't contain him, the staff was afraid of him, and he was running loose with no restraints.

Because I produced his show, I was told (in no uncertain terms) to "get control of Darron and his tendency for outbursts." That was utterly ridiculous! After all, if the people who were cutting his check couldn't control him, how could I? The truth of the matter is that the corporate office needed a scapegoat. Apparently they thought I was white, had horns, and liked to chew on shoe leather, because I was elected. I was fired. Perhaps they thought that someone else might be able to "get control" of Darron. If so, they were wrong. The on air rants continued, and are ongoing even now.

For a while, I was angry, bitter and very upset. I hated Darron for what he'd done to me. More importantly, I hated what I had done to myself. I knew things were bad and getting worse. I was in a toxic environment and, after exercising all the control in my power, I didn't GET OUT. The next 365 days made up the hardest year I had ever experienced. I was broke. I lost my wife. And, I lost the home I made for myself.

Ask for help & accept it graciously.

I spent so much time focusing on all that I had lost that I considered ending my life. I truly believe that the devil was trying to take me out. Luckily, I serve a God who did not create me to destroy myself.

Something told me to pick up the phone and call my friend, Fonzworth Bentley. With tears in my eyes, and no desire to live, I mustered up the strength to say three words, "I need prayer." Bentley asked me what was going on, and I honestly cannot remember what I told him. I do, however, remember what he said to me. "You are here for greater purpose Tazz, and the enemy cannot have you. God takes care of the birds and they don't worry, and you're not going to worry either." We prayed and talked for what seemed like hours. While I don't remember everything, I do remember a great peace coming over my spirit. A true friend, Fonzworth did not give up on me, even when I wanted to give up on myself.

BE a friend.

I can count the times that Fonzworth Bentley and I have been in the same room. Even so, he has always been there for me. So many people think that proximity is the most important thing when it comes to friendship. Those people are sadly mistaken. When I lost my job, Bentley was there with an encouraging word. When I need a favor, Bentley always comes through for me. Even 2000 miles away, he has always been there. That's just one example of true friendship.

True friends will always be there for you when you need them the most – cherish them.

Tazz's Tips: Handling Friends and Haters

- No one person is totally your friend or is totally a hater.
- Understand the on-line-communication barrier. Don't assume – ask.
- Know when to "Get Out" – and do it early!
- Ask for help & accept it graciously.
- BE a friend.

"Never explain--your friends do not need it and your enemies will not believe you anyway."

  - Elbert Hubbard (1856-1915), Writer & Philosopher

Chapter 8:
Surround Yourself with Positive People

Do you keep toxic things next to the nutritious? I'm not talking about the occasional science project in the fridge when you forgot about last week's take out. I'm talking about keeping the Drano^R in the fridge with the food, or in the cabinet right next to the Wheaties^R. No, of course not!

There are all kinds of toxic things in our homes, but hopefully they are needed. Do you keep non-essential toxic items? I hope not. If you live in an apartment or condo with a maintenance man, I doubt you have a can of Drain-O^R. If you have toxic things in your house that are non-essential, throw them out. And that applies to people, too.

Take regular inventory of the people closest to you.

Take stock of the people around you and eliminate those who are not helpful to your mission. Hang on to those who support you morally, emotionally, and psychologically. I can almost guarantee that if you focus on the positive people in your life, you will see amazing results from your hard work.

"Justin" works for one of the biggest law firms in the Dallas-Fort Worth area. Over the period of a few months, we had several deep conversations. During one of these, Justin posed a question that totally changed my life. "Tazz, why are you the smartest person in your group of friends?" Dumbfounded, I had no proper response.

Justin broke it down for me. "Tazz, if you are the smartest person in your group of friends, that means you are the nucleus of the group. The nucleus is the center and everything feeds off of it. This is good for everyone who feeds off of the nucleus, but for the nucleus itself, it's damaging. Tazz, you're not being fed so it's time to change your group." Because Justin could be so real with me, I count him as a true friend. Furthermore, our conversation made me take stock of the people in my group of friends, and I made adjustments accordingly.

Cherish your true friends, and eliminate the ones who do not have your best interests at heart.

True friendships are very hard to come by; but fake friendships and enemies are really easy to make. One of the hardest things a human being can do in life is to differentiate between who's truly a friend, and who is truly there to take advantage of them. Those who are motivated by greed and personal advancement will make "friendships" with you, for whatever goods and services you can provide them. People like this are only in it for what you can give them and will never be there for you when you need them the most.

Perhaps Niccolo Machiavelli's most famous quote is *Keep your friends close and your enemies closer*[5]. I respectfully disagree with this very articulate and brilliant man. I believe that you should keep your friends close and eliminate the enemies from your life. Haters and "fake friends" are toxic people. Having them anywhere around you is just poisoning your spirit, and destroying your objectives.

Eliminate people who try to use you for what you can bring to their life, especially when they don't offer to bring anything into yours.

I've run into many people who befriended me, simply for what I could do for them. "Jimmy" was such an individual.

As an on-air personality, an obsession of any sort can be career suicide. This is especially true for a "negative" obsession – like haters. Jimmy was obsessed with people he felt were haters. He posted things that were said to him or about him on his Facebook wall for everyone to see. Moreover, he spent the first 25 minutes of his show each night addressing his alleged haters. Frankly, I became very concerned for Jimmy's image. Spending time worrying about detractors does not engender respect. It's unprofessional and appears self aggrandizing. After I noticed the pattern, I felt that it was my duty as a friend and colleague to have a heart to heart talk with him.

I was totally flabbergasted by his response. He said, "You've got a lot of advice, yet you've never offered a high-profile celebrity guest for my show."

At that moment, I realized that Jimmy had no interest in me, my views, or being my friend. The lunches, phone calls, and text messages were all red herrings. He had hoped to gain access to my network in the entertainment industry. At this point, my Common Sense kicked in and I cut all ties with him.

The best revenge is ultimate success.

Obsession with haters takes energy away from your goals. You cannot afford to waste time when it comes to achieving your dreams. Every second of your life is a precious resource that you will never see again. Why would you waste your time on people who don't matter to you? Haters can be like leeches, sucking the very life's blood out of you. Use your Common Sense to assure that haters will have no effect on you and your vision.

"No" does not equal "Bad," and "Yes" does not equal "Good."

Here's an eye opener. Ready? I discovered something amazing … everyone who told me "no" wasn't a hater. I also had to learn the corollary … that everyone who told me "yes" wasn't my friend. If you surround yourself with yes-men and yes-women, you are destined to fail in every aspect of human endeavor. If you keep yourself surrounded by a small group of people who truly care about you, it is absolutely certain that you will succeed. Hard work will still be required, but real friends will be there with honest, genuine, practical guidance and advice.

Tazz's Tips: Surrounding Yourself with Positive People

- Take regular inventory of the people closest to you.
- Cherish your true friends, and eliminate the ones who do not have your best interests at heart.
- Eliminate people who try to use you for what you can bring to their life, especially when they don't offer to bring anything into yours.
- The best revenge is ultimate success.
- "No" does not equal "Bad", and "Yes" does not equal "Good."

"Real friendship is shown in times of trouble; prosperity is full of friends."

– Euripedes (480-406 B.C), Playwright

Chapter 9:
Advice from Family

My brother, Aaron, is very street smart. His power of observation is astounding, and he has the uncanny ability to handle any situation, no matter how severe. He may be 7 years older than I, and we may not share a biological father, but closer brothers you will never find.

If I asked to name one person in my life as my hero, without question, that person would be Aaron. When my parents divorced, he acted more like a father to me than he did a brother. Aaron taught me to take care of myself. He used two simple concepts to train me for life. The first was the concept of "The Team."

Remember "The Team."

Aaron's biological father was a living, breathing example of disappointment to him. Some of my earliest memories are of him sitting by the doorstep, waiting for his father to show up. The long awaited arrival never happened. Between my parents' divorce and being disappointed with his biological father, Aaron believed that he could only count on three people: my mother, me, and himself. This was the nucleus of The Team. Frequently, my brother would say to me, "No matter where you go, no matter what you do in life, always remember The Team." My brother believed that, with the support of each other, our family could overcome any obstacle and meet every goal with absolutely no problems. As an adult, I expanded the team concept into my career, and into my circle of friends. It has definitely served me well over the years.

Follow your dream & support the dreams of those around you.

My father, a decorated police officer who spent at least 30 years in law-enforcement, hated the idea of my brother becoming a cop. Even as Alzheimer-related dementia set in, he was adamantly opposed to my brother having a badge. It didn't matter that Aaron had already been on the force for at least eight years. When my father looked at Aaron, he saw his little boy. The idea of Aaron being hurt or killed was a thought that my father could not bear. Even though he didn't agree with Aaron's choices, deep down, I know my father was extremely proud. My brother followed his dream. And, in my humble opinion, Aaron is one of the best police officers Philadelphia has ever had.

Just as Aaron's dream led him to a career my Dad did not think was safe, I didn't choose a career that my brother deemed safe either. "I don't know how you can do it," he said. "The broadcast industry is full of snakes. They are cutthroat, and they will stab you in the back the second they can." I laughed, responding, "Aaron, this is what I was born to do. I love entertaining people and I'm good at it. To be honest, I don't know how *you* do what *you* do! Philadelphia isn't exactly a safe city to be a police officer. There are drug dealers, wannabe gangsters, and crazy people - most of whom are carrying very heavy artillery. I think I picked a safer career."

No doubt my brother might have liked it better if I were a doctor or lawyer. Even so, he has always been incredibly supportive. I can't think of a show I've done where my brother wasn't in attendance. Aaron shows how much he loves and appreciates me by being there for me when I need him the most.

Aaron followed his path, and respects that I have followed my own as well. This is exactly how a family should operate. Unfortunately, this isn't the case for most families. I contend that families should operate from a place of love, but most seem to be ruled from a place of fear.

Don't let other people's fear & jealousy drive your behavior.

People have all kinds of fears related to watching you pursue your dreams.

- A parent's fear of their child growing up in a world for which they are not prepared,
- The fear of potential financial disaster (due to life and career choices that you may make),
- The fear of seeing you fail, and
- Sometimes, the fear of seeing you succeed.

Yes, you read that correctly: the fear of seeing you succeed. What a crazy concept! People who share your DNA, may actually be jealous or afraid that you could become a success. My mother says, "Many people don't mind you doing well, as long as you don't do better than they are." It's a sad, hurtful statement; but, it's a statement that has proven time and again to be dreadfully accurate. I'm not saying that every family member in your life is trying to hate on you directly. I'm saying that a lot of people are not happy with the choices they've made in their lives, so they want to try and live vicariously through you. Some may want to place the limits that they've experienced in their lives on you. This behavior is toxic and, if you allow it, can easily kill your dreams.

Pursue your dreams as far as you possibly can. Never let anyone talk you out of something about which you feel passionate.

A few years ago, my niece, Kiarra, scraped her knee. Her mother, Trish, immediately cleaned it up, applied some Neosporin®, and finished the first-aid with a Band-Aid® and a kiss. Immediately, Kiarra felt "all better." That's when the idea of a lifetime hit my brain! Excitedly I said to my family, "I have a million dollar idea! What if I made Band-Aid®'s that have Neosporin® already in them? I could call them 'Achy-Aids'!! They could even feature different cartoon characters!" My family looked at me like I was crazy, and then burst into uproarious laughter. Their remarks convinced me that the idea would never work, so I didn't bother to pursue it any further.

Several months later I was watching television, when a commercial came on. The Band-Aid® brand came out with a piece of bandage that had Neosporin® already in them! All at once, I was angry and disappointed with myself. Why didn't I pursue something that I knew in my heart could have been profitable? Because I held on to my family's laughter and felt immediately discouraged. I called my sister-in-law to inform her and my family that my idea was on the market by Band-Aid®. Neither she, nor my other family members laughed at the idea again. I don't really blame my family for discouraging me, but I do blame myself for not following my instincts. My family didn't mean any harm; they just didn't think my idea had merit. I learned several lessons from the Achy-Aids incident:

- Not everyone will value, appreciate, or understand your vision.
- Always follow your first instincts. They almost never steer you in the wrong direction.
- If your family does not have a certain level of expertise in your area of pursuit, take their advice and criticism with a grain of salt. Then find experts to help you with your goals.
- The only thing worse than failing at something that you attempt, is to never attempt it at all.
- The universe has a way of getting what it wants with or without you. If you do not pursue a dream, the universe will find someone else to pursue it without you!
- A family's affect on one's psyche is a very delicate thing. Their words, support, or lack thereof can make-or-break you in every aspect of your life.

It's very easy to encourage someone when they're already successful. You can readily see the results of their effort. It is much more difficult and very brave to support someone while the person is still pursuing their path.

You can choose your friends but not your family. Families are a mixed bag of emotions of love, jealousy, and insecurity. While some family members have a wealth of knowledge and wisdom, others suffer from an over abundance of stupidity.

It is up to you to sort through the advice and thoughts that they give you, and make the best possible decisions for your life. One thing is certain: only you will reap the consequences and repercussions of your choices. I hope you choose wisely.

Tazz's Tips: Dealing with Family Members and Their "Advice"

- Remember "The Team."
- Follow your dream & support the dreams of those around you.
- Don't let other people's fear & jealousy drive your behavior.
- Pursue your dreams as far as you possibly can. Never let anyone talk you out of something about which you feel passionate.

"Advice is like snow; the softer it falls, the longer it dwells upon, and the deeper it sinks into, the mind."

 – Samuel Taylor Coleridge (1772–1834), Philosopher

Chapter 10:
Determination Is the Key Factor in Your Success

Increase your Circle.

In the last chapter, I told you that my brother Aaron taught me two concepts that have served me well. We've already touched on The Team. The second is a concept by which my brother swears, "The Circle."

I'm not sure where Aaron came up with The Circle, but it totally changed my life. As a teenager, although I was gifted, I was also troubled. I wasn't robbing liquor stores, doing drugs, or getting girls pregnant. I just wasn't acclimated to being around kids my own age. While I attended a normal public high school, that was the extent of what I had in common with my peers. I worked at a radio station and my parents were significantly older than those of most teenagers. My views and thoughts about the world were different than most people my age. Combine that with the fact that my hormones were raging out of control, and I was frustrated with just about every aspect of my life. My mother truly had a lot with which to contend.

I'm sure Aaron saw it in my mother's eyes. The roiling annoyance, irritation, disappointment, longing, anxiety, apprehension and insecurity that makes up teenage angst. And the resulting drain of energy from trying to deal with me. All it took was one look, and he took matters into his own hands. He called me into the kitchen for a chat. "I understand your frustration," he acknowledged. "It seems like Mom doesn't understand you right now, and the kids at the school don't understand you; but trust me when I tell you that I do. The truth of the matter is, aside from getting good grades and doing what you love, you really don't have much else to do. All Mom wants is for you to be responsible; and, while she won't give you the freedom that you want right now, one day very soon she will."

"You see, life is like a circle," he said as he stretched his hand toward me. He extended his fingers and kept his palm parallel to the ground. He then began to move his hands in a small circular motion. "The more you look competent in life, the more you'll receive. At first it will be small things, like a later curfew, and more privacy. Later on, your hard work will increase your circle. All the things you ever wanted like a car, a house, and success will come to you as a result of your maturity, work ethic, and determination. One day you'll look back at this conversation and realize that your brother was right. Your circle will continue to increase as long as you stay determined to do everything possible to make your circle bigger."

I honestly don't know if he was setting out to become a major influence on my life, or if he was trying to prevent me from becoming a snot-nosed brat. Whatever the reason, my brother imbued me with a spirit of determination. My hero, I work hard every day to make him proud to say that I'm his brother.

Resolve to achieve excellence at any cost.

I cannot talk about determination without mentioning one of my greatest mentors, Wendy Williams. As long as I've been alive, I've never known anyone like her. I had the pleasure of working with Wendy as a much younger man. To be honest, I was scared to death. The shadow of Wendy Williams loomed large over the broadcasting industry – and little of it was good. As I got to know her, I realized that being a woman with determination is one of the hardest things you can be in this world. Most people will classify you as a bitch.

One evening Wendy told me something that would change my life. She said, "Tazz, in order to succeed in this business, you must be prepared to do anything. A lot of people see me now but they don't understand what I went through for so many years in order to get to where I am today. I loved this business so much that I took a job in the US Virgin Islands making only $25 a week. If you want to be successful, you have to be both determined and willing to make the sacrifices necessary in order to get to the top."

I couldn't believe what I was hearing! I couldn't picture the great Wendy Williams living off of $25 a week in the US Virgin Islands - just to be on the radio. I also could not grasp the concept of leaving Philadelphia. Philly is a major market. I had done well for myself, but I felt that I wasn't getting the respect I deserved.

After mulling it over, I decided to leave Power 99 and make my mark as an unknown radio personality in a small market. I figured that if Wendy could survive off $25 a week,

I could surely survive off $20,000 a year in Fayetteville, North Carolina. On my last day, Wendy said, "The next time I see you, I expect you to be successful." With that kind of endorsement, my determination and resolve to be the best only grew stronger.

Eight years later, I was producing the Rickey Smiley Morning Show, which became the fastest growing morning show in the country at the time. I was beyond excited when Wendy came to town promoting her new daytime TV talk show. I hadn't seen her since our conversation in Philadelphia!

When she arrived in the studio, she gave me a huge hug and told me how proud she was of me. When she went on the air, she told the cast how she always tried to be a help to the young, and that I was one of her success stories. I was so touched; I almost broke down and cried.

Resolve to achieve excellence at any cost. Wendy gave me some excellent advice. My Common Sense kicked in, and I took action. You need to do the same. This includes overcoming the obstacles you place on yourself. I overcame my reluctance to leave Philadelphia, and there were other self-induced obstacles to overcome along the way too.

Face your insecurities head on.

It is very hard to face your own insecurities. I've only had a few, but one of the biggest has been my weight. To this day, I fluctuate up and down, having a constant fight with the scale and the fast food drive-thru window. When my father died, I became a lot more selective in choosing what I put into my body. Even still, the Battle of the Bulge has taken its toll. The cost has been paid in the battering of my psyche.

As a kid, people teased me. As an adult, it was the

only insult that people could hurl at me. They couldn't talk about my career, my love life, or my happiness. All they could say was that I was fat. I'm not going say that it didn't hurt, because I'd be lying to you. After a while, I heard it so much that two things happened. First, I began to believe it. This led to several bad choices in my eating habits. I believed that I was fat; therefore I would always be fat. Second, the insults stopped bothering me. I reached a different conclusion. *That's really the best anyone can do to attack me? Well, then the rest of me must be pretty awesome!* I made a choice. I decided that my weight would never stop me from achieving anything. Simply put, I resolved to achieve everything I set my mind to accomplish. As a result, my "Circle" expanded.

Energy is real and tangible. Be mindful of the energy that you put out, as well as the energy that you allow into your personal space.

There is no "magic pill" for success. If there were, there would be no need for this book. Everything that happens to you is a direct result of the energy you radiate. Some of you probably think I'm absolutely crazy for saying that; but it's the truth.

Have you ever been around a person who's always smiling and has a positive outlook on life? I bet you can tell whether or not that person is genuine within 5 seconds. Did you ever stop to wonder how, without knowing their current situation, you're able to discern the genuinely happy people from the ones who are faking it? It's because of the energy they radiate!

Some people equate *energy* with a *feeling, vibe,* or having a *sixth sense.* It all means the same thing. And it applies directly to business. Let's use gambling as an example. Watch what happens when a table gets "hot" (meaning that people are beginning to win at an alarming rate). The pit boss (a manager hired by the casino to watch the floor) replaces the dealer. Why? He is hoping to change the energy of the players at the table. People are capable of generating enough power, simply by feeling one way or another, that it can affect everyone around them.

As a standup comedian, I've worked plenty of stages all across the country. When I first started out, I bombed - really badly! A lot of it had to do with my nervous energy. My material was solid, my delivery was good, but my nerves got the better of me. That's just strange. Being a standup comedian requires that you stand up in front of people! I'm not a particularly shy person, and never have been. Strangely enough, there were times when I was petrified of being on the stage; and it showed. Once I learned to control my energy, everything opened up for me.

In order to be successful, you must be determined in everything that you set out to accomplish. Insecurities and The Doubt Monster will constantly try to attack you; don't let them win. You control your own destiny. To think otherwise, would be to set out on the path to certain failure. You cannot let that happen!

Tazz's Tips: Mastering the Art of Determination

- Increase your Circle.
- Resolve to achieve excellence at any cost.
- Face your insecurities head on.
- Energy is real and tangible. Be mindful of the energy that you put out, as well as the energy that you allow into your personal space.

"Nothing in this world can take the place of persistence. Talent will not; nothing is more common than unsuccessful people with talent. Genius will not; unrewarded genius is almost a proverb. Education will not; the world is full of educated derelicts. Persistence and determination alone are omnipotent. The slogan 'press on' has solved, and always will solve, the problems of the human race."

   –Calvin Coolidge (1872-1933), 30th President of the
    United States

Chapter 11:
Responsibility

Share your knowledge, share your insights, and share your perspective. We all have a responsibility to make our mark, leaving the world a better place.

Not all determination should be about you.

After only eight months of courtship, my grandparents were married. To hear my grandfather tell it, before he could blink an eye there were six amazing children running around the house.

In those days, it was traditional for the husband to be the sole breadwinner, and Pop-Pop was determined to provide a great life for his family. As a result of this determination, he obtained a position working for the Budd Company. In very little time, my grandfather became one of their first Black welders. While that may not sound like a big deal, it was extremely unusual in the 1940's. (In case you're wondering why a brewery needed a welder, it's not that "Budd." The

Budd Company, established in 1912, supplies metal parts to the automobile industry.)

He could have been satisfied with having that high-paying welding job and taking care of his family. Instead, he trained some of his friends and neighbors. He prepared them to work with him at the Budd Company. My grandfather's actions are a clear example of why not all determination should be about you. You should be determined to help your friends and family grow, develop, and reach their dreams as well. The energy you create while doing so is powerful and tangible!

It would be easy to think that my grandfather had very few financial issues, but nothing could be further from the truth. The automotive industry was as unstable back then as it is now. Pop-Pop faced a great number of layoffs and setbacks, but he never let that deter him. My grandfather's determination still inspires me.

Determination Requires Discipline.

When I was about six or seven years of age, Pop-Pop decided that he was going to take me under his wing. After coming home from school, my grandfather made sure I completed all of my homework. He even checked it for mistakes and errors. While my grandfather did not have a formal education, he read everything he could. If there was a way to get his hands on a book, he made it his business to make that happen. His favorite book was the Bible, and he read it to me on a regular basis.

After homework and scriptures, my grandfather took me to his garage and he taught me what I would need to know in order to be a good man. I learned how to change oil, mix cement, and lay brick. None of this interested me! I remember asking him, "Pop-Pop, why are you showing me all this stuff?" He smiled at me and said, "Because you need to know, and it will keep you out of trouble. Look at your mother, aunts, and uncles. All of them are educated, and absolutely none of them are criminals. Without discipline there can be no determination. You'll need all the discipline you can get to be successful growing up in the world as it is today." In my heart and mind, I totally believe that my grandfather's philosophies were the epitome of Common Sense.

Choose your goals wisely. A determination mindset comes with a heavy level of responsibility.

If you are determined to be the head of a Fortune 500 company, you must make sure that you have the necessary education and training. There's nothing negative about having a lofty goal. Just remember to choose wisely. If the goal itself is negative, you will experience all the pitfalls and drama that are associated with that objective.

I have watched so many of my peers, as well as the generation behind me, get caught up in what they believe is the glamorous Hustler/Drug Dealer lifestyle. Watch any rap video. The cash on hand, Aston Martins - on the surface it seems desirable. Most of them fail to realize where that lifestyle leads. It can only lead to two definite ends: prison or an untimely death. No one in the media likes to talk about that aspect of it. After all, it does not increase ratings.

I'm not knocking anyone's hustle, or the way they choose to live their lives. As a kid who grew up in the hood, I've seen the worst of what life has to offer. As an adult in corporate America and mainstream entertainment, I've also seen the best of what life has to offer. I've seen people take businesses from absolutely nothing and build them into empires. I don't know about you, but I would rather build an empire (one which is legal and safe) than to try to become the next Tony Montana, Big Meech, or Larry Hoover. The only thing those gentlemen have in common is an unhappy ending to their stories. I'm determined to live a life that is long and prosperous. Decide what your goals are and fuel yourself with the energy of determination in order to make them happen.

Tazz's Tips: Being Responsible

- Not all determination should be about you.
- Determination requires Discipline.
- Choose your goals wisely. A determination mindset comes with a heavy level of responsibility.

"Provision for others is a fundamental responsibility of human life."

   -Woodrow Wilson (1856-1924), 28th President of the United States

Chapter 12:
The Microwave Mentality

Society has become ruled by people's desire for instantaneous gratification. Our patience is pretty much a thing of the past. I call this the "Microwave Mentality."

Capitalize on discoveries.

The microwave oven came about, like most things in this life do, by timing - when it was least expected. During the Second World War, two scientists invented something called the magnetron. The magnetron was a tube that produced microwaves. The microwaves were used to spot Nazi warplanes on their way to bomb the British Isles. This was one of the first forms of radar.

Sometime in the future, Percy LeBaron Spencer discovered that the radiation melted a candy bar in his pocket. This prompted several experiments showing that microwaves could raise the temperature of foods a lot quicker than a conventional oven.

Plan, prepare, research, and then track progress as you MAKE IT HAPPEN.

Eleven years later, in 1954, the Raytheon Company went to market with the first commercially available microwave oven. Named "The Radar Range," it was so bulky and expensive that only restaurants and hotels carried one. The early version of the present day microwave oven wasn't developed and marketed to consumers until 1967.

The microwave oven took a long time to develop into what it is today. It took a lot of planning, preparation, research, and careful execution to make it safe and marketable. One of the greatest icons for time-saving took well over 20 years to develop into a viable product.

This means that you have to take your time with whatever it is you want to accomplish. Don't be scared or hesitant; just make sure that you have everything you need in order to achieve your goals. That includes a plan, the necessary knowledge/education, and the willingness to see it through to the end.

Don't get trapped in a "quick fix".

In 1984, my mother bought a new microwave oven. It wasn't anything like the microwaves we have today. This thing was big, noisy, and bulky! My brother seemed to know everything about how microwave ovens worked. I had absolutely no clue, but was intrigued when Aaron informed me that food could be cooked in less time than it would take to cook something in a conventional oven.

From that point forward, I was obsessed with the microwave. I made my mother's morning coffee, heated bologna for lunch, and prepared frozen pizzas for dinner

- all in the microwave. I think this was the onset of my impatience becoming such a problem. I always wanted to get things done quickly, that way I could do whatever I wanted to do. But it didn't always work out that way. I can remember several occasions when I thought a sandwich was hot and, in reality, it was ice cold on the inside. This meant that I used the microwave again in order to heat the food completely, which cost more time. Suddenly my "convenience" was becoming more of an inconvenience than anything else. On top of that, while microwave ovens can be convenient and save time, the food does not seem to have the care, love, and finesse that it does when prepared by conventional means.

Remember that everything happens in its own time! Don't rush the process; embrace it!

Although I went through the microwave stage, my mother's love of cooking was infused into my life. She taught me to cook full-blown meals at the age of seven. Mom said it would prepare me for becoming a good husband. Secretly, I think she taught me how to cook so that I could cook for her. Whatever her reason, her passion for creating culinary masterpieces became my own.

My signature dish is called "Tazz Daddy's Sweet and Heat Texas Chili." The secret recipe takes at least five hours to prepare. My nephew could not understand why something as simple as a meal would take so long. I explained that making a good pot of chili includes quality ingredients, the time you spend preparing it, and the love that goes into it. When my family tasted it for the first time, they were absolutely speechless! They couldn't believe how good it was.

After his third bowl, AJ remarked, "Now I understand why it takes five hours!"

I highly recommend that you live your life the way I make my chili. Take your time and enjoy the full experience of everything that life has to offer you. I am in no way implying that all you need to do is tiptoe through the proverbial tulips. However, I feel very strongly that we rush through so many aspects of our lives that we miss the whole of our experience by focusing on the sum of its parts. Experience it, pay attention, focus on it, and make sure you don't miss any steps. Opportunities for a GREAT chili are lost by skipping a step or forgetting the secret ingredient. Opportunities can be lost in other areas of your life by making the same types of unnecessary mistakes.

Utilize your Common Sense to prevent unnecessary mistakes.

In 2004, I purchased a used Buick Century, Limited Edition. I really loved that car, but the wear and tear of time took its toll, and I needed a new vehicle. I purchased a Jeep Cherokee and was extremely happy.

I put off selling the Buick. I noticed it had a flat tire, but put off fixing that too. My apartment complex had a policy about flat tires and abandoned cars. If you didn't fix a flat tire, they hired a towing company to take your car away. Wrapped up in my brand-new SUV, I hadn't even noticed that the car had been towed. Needless to say, the fees for holding onto the vehicle had become astronomical, and it would cost more than the vehicle was worth in order to get it back.

I could have easily fixed the tire and sold the Buick, netting a very nice profit. But, instead of practicing Common

Sense, I employed the Microwave Mentality. This led me to move on with my Jeep before I finished with the Buick. In essence, I made an unconscious decision to lose my Buick. And it didn't have to happen.

Identify the things that you can't control. Focus on what you can control.

Human beings seem to feel that controlling every aspect of our lives will guarantee safety, happiness, and success. Nothing could be further from the truth. You can control yourself, and the decisions that you make; but there are things at work all around us with a timetable that has nothing at all to do with us.

If you wanted an apple, you could take some apple seeds and plant them, controlling several aspects of that decision. You decide how many seeds to plant and where to plant them. You control how often you water them and whether or not you give them plant food. But, no matter how much you control some things, you cannot control the outcome. Regardless of what you do, you cannot control which seeds take root or how long it takes for that apple tree to grow. And whether or not the fruit will be edible? You most certainly cannot control that either.

Follow through.

There are approximately 6,000,000,000 people on the earth right now. Aside from those who may have mental difficulties, we all have ideas. Some of the ideas we have are original, while some are shared. Some are as simple as *"I want to make some chili."* Some are more complicated, like *"I want to build a car that can drive on land as well as underwater."* What separates a thought that goes on to become something tangible, from a thought that becomes a memory? A person's ability to follow through and stick with it until it develops fully. Some people will take an idea all the way, while others will scrap it at the first sign of adversity. In order to live a very successful life, one that is filled with purpose and success, you must be willing and able to see your ideas all the way through. Otherwise, you're no different than the billions of other people on planet Earth who never achieve their full potential. Be patient, be diligent, and go after your future with a deliberate mentality - not a Microwave Mentality.

Tazz's Tips: Overcoming the Microwave Mentality

- Capitalize on discoveries.
- Plan, prepare, research, and track progress as you MAKE IT HAPPEN.
- Don't get trapped in a "quick fix."
- Remember that everything happens in its own time! Don't rush the process, embrace it!
- Utilize your Common Sense to prevent unnecessary mistakes.
- Identify the things that you can't control. Focus on what you can control.
- Follow through.

"Commitment is what transforms a promise into reality. It is the words that speak boldly of your intentions. And the actions which speak louder than the words. It is making the time when there is none. Coming through time after time after time, year after year after year. Commitment is the stuff character is made of; the power to change the face of things. It is the daily triumph of integrity over skepticism."

- Abraham Lincoln (1809–1865), 16th President of the United States.

Chapter 13:
You Get What You Dream

I don't know about anyone else, but I've always had a high level of expectation for myself. I've always viewed my life as some grand adventure; one that would always take me to places I could only imagine. My mother was big on making sure that I understood the power of having a great imagination.

Explore. Learn.

Before the market was flooded with all kinds of developmental toys for children, my mother made it her business to make sure that I could read everything I got my hands on, and that I had plenty of creative outlets to express myself. My mother went out of her way to find things that she knew would intrigue me. She found book-on-tape adaptations of my favorite cartoons and movies, and got me in the habit of reading along with them in order to further develop my vocabulary.

Language is one of the most essential things in

getting what you want out of life. If you are capable of communicating effectively, you hold the power to make your dreams come true. As a teacher, I think a lot of what my mother did came out of a natural instinct and love for education. As a mother, I know that she just wanted to make sure I had the best upbringing possible so that I could take on a world that didn't really care about me.

Take care; but don't let fear rob you of experiences.

My father was the kind of person who wanted to make it perfectly clear to me that the world was a dangerous place. As I watched my brother follow in my father's footsteps as both a father and officer of the law, I can totally understand how a career in law-enforcement can make anyone paranoid. It was my father's caution/paranoia that created one of my first memories as a child.

As a kid I had a steady diet of programs like Sesame Street and Mr. Rogers' Neighborhood. I always thought it was amazing that Mr. Rogers had an entire magical land of make-believe with characters, stories and a trolley that ran through his home. He was my hero, second only to my father in my heart.

One day my father strapped me into the car seat of his big Cadillac as we travelled to the Harrisburg International Airport to pick up my Uncle George. Once my father spotted him, they proceeded to the baggage claim to grab his luggage. I held my father's hand, happy to be accompanying him on a mission, until suddenly I broke away from him. My father hadn't noticed because he was busy removing bags from the conveyor belt.

It had only been a moment, but a moment was all it took to send my father into a tailspin. He began to search frantically for me calling my name, but there was no response. It was then that my father turned around, and he spotted me with a man at the baggage claim kiosk maybe 30 feet away from him. He sprang into action before my uncle had a chance to stop him and ran to the man shaking my hand. With one hand on his police issued weapon, he asked the man to step away from me slowly. The man complied, and very calmly explained himself to my father at the same time. He told my father that I ran up to him, and that it wasn't uncommon for children to do so, simply because they felt safe in his presence. Fueled by adrenaline, concern, and anger, my father was infuriated at this man until I said to him, "Daddy, why are you mad at Mr. Rogers?"

My father's normally chocolate complexion turned beet red with embarrassment. He apologized profusely to Mr. Rogers, and then they both had a good laugh. Immediately, my uncle, my father and Mr. Rogers began to explain to me why it was so important that I'd never run away from the adult who was in charge of taking care of me at the time. From that day forward I never departed from my caretakers.

Isn't it funny that as a three-year-old, all I saw was the man who exposed me to the beauty of imagination, while my father saw a possible kidnapper? Of course, a parent should always err on the side of caution, but it shows you that because of their experiences, adults tend to believe the worst before they can imagine the best. If we had a little more childlike innocence, imagine how many more dreams we would be unafraid to pursue.

Support is precious.

I can't recall a time when my mother discouraged me from anything that I wanted to do. When I was 10 years old I developed a passion for skateboarding. By my 11th birthday, my mother had given me a professional skateboard, subscriptions to popular skateboarding magazines, and all the support a kid could ask for. The truth of the matter is my mother was scared to death that I would break my leg, but she never let me see her concern. Skateboarding turned out to be a lot of fun for me, but it was simply a passing phase. And that was okay with Mom, too.

Being a child of the '80s, I was blessed enough to experience extracurricular activities during my school year. I immediately fell in love with art class. I think most creative people love to draw or doodle, but I was an above average doodler! For the first half of the school year we had a very nice art teacher. She was encouraging, patient, and extremely helpful in trying to teach inner-city children how to develop a technique. Unfortunately, she left in the middle of the school year and was replaced by a person who truly did not know or care about children.

Nothing was ever good enough for my new art teacher. He ripped everything I did to shreds on a consistent basis. That's not a metaphor! He literally ripped my paintings, drawings and sketches to shreds. How someone can do that to a child is beyond my level of comprehension.

Because children are conditioned to believe that teachers are good people who only have your best interests in mind, I began to believe that my artwork was trash because my teacher said so. I was understandably hurt and upset, and I guess that's what my grandfather picked up on when he asked me what was bothering me. I explained to him how my teacher treated my works of art. Instead of marching up to the school and raising a fuss, my grandfather focused on me.

He asked me to draw him something; anything that I felt like. To be honest with you, I don't remember what I drew him, but I do remember him being very impressed. He said to me, "People will always try to discourage you in this life. It's up to you to decide whether or not you're going to let them. If you have a dream of being a great artist, dream that dream, then wake up and make it happen! You've got talent; you just have to develop it. All you need to do is work on your art for at least one hour every day. It may not seem like much, but over a period of time you'll find that you'll get better and better."

It was as if my grandfather had opened me up and inserted a battery into my back. From that point forward I went to school, and I no longer dreaded art class. I ignored my art teachers' negative comments, and I worked on the sketches and paintings that made me happy. Shortly after, the art teacher mysteriously left the school. I don't know if he got fired, nor do I care. I dreamed of one day getting respect and admiration for what I created with my own two hands. Exactly one year after that teacher left the school, I took second place in a citywide art contest for my portrait of the Reverend Dr. Martin Luther King, Jr.

Make a memory.

There were many times I remember my mother being very sad, but putting on a brave face so that I didn't worry about her. I know that taking care of two growing boys is no easy task on a fixed income, but my mother made it look easy. If my brother and I had a want, she supplied it. Mom could make something as trivial as going to the lake to feed stale bread to some ducks into a magical adventure. She called this concept "making a memory."

The point of making a memory is to create something so powerful that it overshadows all the bad things are happening to you when you look over your life in hindsight. I remember days of my mother having to run an extension cord from the neighbor's house to ours because we didn't have power. I remember my mother having to boil hot water so my brother and I could take a bath because the water heater was broken. While those experiences have not totally escaped me, they were never traumatic to me, because I was constantly surrounded by love.

Keep it moving.

It's also important to know that my mother never panicked in front of us. She simply kept it moving. As an adult, I now know that there were several nights that she cried herself to sleep, but she held on to her dreams. My mother saved her money and purchased a hair salon. She did an incredible amount of business simply by word-of-mouth. My mother also got us out of the hood and into a condominium in the northeast section of Philadelphia. She dreamed big dreams, and then she woke up and made them happen.

Folks may not appreciate your dreams. That doesn't change fate.

Dreams are a very funny thing. They can be weird, comical, inspiring, or sometimes wet. Most importantly, they can be prophetic. The problem with your dreams is that people may not understand or appreciate their significance in your heart.

The Bible talks about this in the book of Genesis, with the story of Joseph.

For those of you who aren't Biblical scholars, Jacob had other sons, but favored Joseph (primarily because Joseph was born in the twilight of Jacob's life).

As the story goes, Jacob gave Joseph a coat of many colors, which did little to help his brother's growing disdain for their youngest sibling. They hated him and refused to say a kind word to him. Also, Joseph had two dreams that he shared with his brothers. In the first, he said that he and his brothers were binding sheaves of wheat and while Joseph's sheaf stood tall, his brothers' sheaves bowed down to it. In the other dream, the sun and moon and eleven stars were bowing down to him. This set in motion a plot that would ultimately make Joseph's prophetic and metaphoric dreams become a reality.

Joseph's brothers wound up tricking him and selling him into slavery. This became the first step in his journey and Joseph wound up being a trusted adviser to the Pharoah. He interpreted dreams, and also helped the Pharoah's subjects with their concerns and problems. Ironically, when his family's crops were experiencing some difficulty they sought help from the Pharoah and wound up being referred to Joseph. Just as Joseph's dream prophesized, they all had to kneel before him.

This teaches me quite a few things: first, you can't share your dreams with everyone, because they will not appreciate or understand them. Second, there is always a bigger plan at work, and as long as you keep a very positive attitude about your circumstances and what it is you wish to attain, you will succeed in life.

Dream without limits.

"So, Tazz," you may be thinking, "what do I need to do to gain the kind of success that I need in order to have a happy life?" Thank you for asking! You're going to have to learn to dream without limits. So many people compartmentalize their dreams and ambitions into such tiny boxes, that they leave little room for growth and expansion.

Your imagination is the one place where you can do amazing and seemingly impossible things! You should take full advantage of this fact. Don't simply say "I just want to make enough money to be okay." Tell yourself, with authority, "I want money to be the least of my worries! I want the kind of lifestyle where I can pursue every single dream that I possibly can conceive!"

Tazz's Tips: Getting Your Dreams

- Explore. Learn.
- Take care; but don't let fear rob you of experiences.
- Support is precious.
- Make a memory.
- Keep it moving.
- Folks may not appreciate your dreams. That doesn't change fate.
- Dream without limits.

"If one advances confidently in the direction of his dreams, and endeavors to live the life which he has imagined, he will meet with success unexpected in common hours."

- Henry David Thoreau (1817–1862), Poet, Abolitionist, Critic, Philosopher, Transcendentalist

A Final Message from Tazz

If you dream like you live, and you're living very modestly, how do you ever expect to expand and grow? You have no idea of the things that you're capable of accomplishing! You have absolutely nothing to lose and everything to gain. Take the canvas of your dreams and paint it with the colors of unlimited possibility.

Common Sense, when utilized properly, can help you live a life that is greater than your wildest dreams. You simply have to know how to use it. It's my sincere hope that you're excited, focused, energized, and have a new clarity that can only come from knowing how to practically apply Common Sense.

This is your time! This is your moment! Seize it! You can do it! All it takes is a little Common Sense! Now get out there, and MAKE THINGS HAPPEN!

References:

1- Dictionary.com, http://dictionary.com

2- ibid

3- ibid

4- ibid

5- Niccolo Machiavelli, <u>The Prince</u>, 1532.

Award winning Radio Personality, Comedian, Author and Speaker, Tazz Daddy has spent most of his life viewing and experiencing the ups and downs of the entertainment industry. He brings an up-close look to the best and worst applications of common sense. A proud Temple University Alumnus, Tazz resides in Philadelphia.

CPSIA information can be obtained at www.ICGtesting.com
Printed in the USA
BVOW031133240213

314060BV00001B/38/P